EARLY CHILDHOOD EDUCATION
AND CHILD CARE

Challenges and Opportunities for America's Public Schools

Anne Bridgman

AMERICAN ASSOCIATION OF SCHOOL ADMINISTRATORS

Early Childhood Education and Child Care, Copyright ©1989, American Association of School Administrators, Arlington, Virginia.

Design by Optima Design, Inc.
Cover Illustration by Sharon Cohen.

Library of Congress Catalog Card Number: 89-83986
ISBN: 0-87652-139-1
AASA Stock Number: 021-00251

Points of view or opinions expressed in this book are those of the authors and do not necessarily represent the official position of AASA.

Additional copies of this publication and others may be ordered from AASA Publications, 1801 N. Moore St., Arlington, Virginia 22209-9988; (703) 528-0700. Price lists and catalogs are available on request.

AASA is an Equal Opportunity Employer.

Foreword

Our civilization ultimately will be measured, in large part, by how we treat our young children. The youngest in any nation are often the first to be adversely affected by changing social, political, and economic conditions. On the other hand, these children are curious, ready to learn, and bursting with energy.

This book, *Early Childhood Education and Child Care: Challenges and Opportunities for America's Public Schools,* will help schools and communities answer many compelling questions as they seek to deal with this growing need in our society. The pressure is increasing to push academic performance on children even before they enter kindergarten. Is that appropriate? The need for child care is burgeoning. What is the school's role? Somehow, early childhood education and child care services must be paid for. Who will pick up the check? Services for children should meet the highest standards. Who should set those standards and what should they be?

Demographic projections show the intensity of need. For example, by 1995, the U.S. Census Bureau predicts that 73 percent of all children under age 18 and 80 percent of children under age six will have mothers working outside the home. During the mid-1980s, already 20 percent of white children and 59 percent of black children under 18 lived in single-parent families. In short, early childhood education and child care are issues that schools and society simply cannot ignore. If we do, we do so at our own peril.

The American Association of School Administrators (AASA) is grateful to the many school leaders across North America who responded to our survey for this book and who shared examples of effective programs. We also want to acknowledge the early childhood education and child care experts whose work has contributed to this publication.

If we wish to see the future, all we need to do is look into the eyes of our children. They are our future, and they need us now.

Richard D. Miller
Executive Director
American Association of School Administrators

Table of Contents

i **FOREWORD**

vii **INTRODUCTION**
   viii The Questions—The Concerns
    ix Some Answers

1 **CHAPTER 1: The Background, the Research, the Debate**
    1 The Demographic Picture
        Working Women and Their Children
        Changes in the Family
        Children in Poverty

    4 The Research
        The Benefits
        The Concerns

   11 The Debate
        The Debate over Sponsorship
        Challenges to School Responsibility
        Counterpoints
        Ensuring Quality
        A Growing Necessity

   20 Where to Start

23 **CHAPTER 2: What Are Early Childhood Programs?**
   24 The Range of Early Childhood and Child Care Programs
        Self-Care
        In-Home Care By Others
        Family Day Care
        Nursery Schools
        Child Care Centers
        Head Start
        Infant and Toddler Care
        Kindergarten
        Other Kindergarten Program Alternatives
        Programs for Handicapped Children
        Programs for the Gifted and Talented

Extended-Day Care
Other Public School Programs
Employer-Sponsored Child Care

38 **Funding Early Childhood Programs**
Federal Funds
State's Role
Local Funding
Funding By Parents
Private Contributions

44 **Licensing and Regulation in Preschool Programs**
State Licensing Standards
Other Standards

49 CHAPTER 3: The Nuts and Bolts of Preschool Programs

50 **Program Structure**
Format
Curriculum
Length of Day
Class Size
Age Grouping
Facility Design
Written Policies

64 **Program Components**
Health and Safety
Insuring Early Childhood Programs
Nutrition
Language Development
Parental Involvement
Multicultural Issues
Grading and Assessment
Discipline
Materials and Equipment

85 CHAPTER 4: Developmental Appropriateness: What It Is, Why It's Important

The Pitfalls of Inappropriateness
Pressure for Academics

88 **What Is "Developmentally Appropriate"?**
Child Development and How Children Learn

90 **How Do You Design a Developmentally Appropriate Curriculum?**
Developmental Versus Chronological Age
Consider Age Versus Individual Appropriateness
Ensuring Developmental Appropriateness

94 **Evaluating Children Developmentally**

        Screening and Readiness Testing
        Concerns About Testing
        Some Evaluation Methods that Work

  100 What School Leaders Can Do

103 CHAPTER 5: Children's Caregivers: Early Childhood Staff

  103 Who Staffs Preschool Programs? Teachers/Caregivers

  105 Conditions in the Field
        Low Pay, Few Benefits
        High Turnover

  107 Training and Certification
        General Qualifications
        Recommended Curricula
        Teaching Early Childhood Education Versus Elementary Studies
        Staff Development, Inservice Training

  116 Ongoing Concerns
        Improvements Hindered

  118 A Final Note

121 CHAPTER 6: The Importance of Parental Involvement

  122 Benefits to All

  122 Effective Cooperation
        Written Communication
        Daily Contact, Regular Participation

  127 Parenting Skills

  128 Family Services

  130 Involving Parents in the Total Educational Spectrum
        Barriers to Involvement

133 CHAPTER 7: Getting Started: How To Establish a Program

  134 Step One: The Needs Assessment
        Contact Existing Providers
        Research Parents' Needs
        Begin To Define the Program

  139 Step Two: Forming a Committee
        Invite Representatives
        Define Charge and Timeframe
        Publicize the Formation of the Committee and Proceedings

140   Step Three: The Committee's Work
        Honing Program Definition
        Rules and Regulations
        Funding and Other Money Matters
        Children
        Teachers
        Parents
        Program Site and Components
        The School and Community Framework
        Troubleshooting

151   Step Four: Winning Approval

151   Step Five: Spreading the Word

155   CHAPTER 8: Maintaining a High Quality Program

156   Day-to-Day Management
        Consistent Funding a Necessity
        The Benefits of Regular Evaluation
        Acting on the Results

165   CHAPTER 9: Options and Recommendations for the 1990's and Beyond

166   One Option: Community Schools

167   Another Option: Public Schools as Providers

168   Other Options

170   Recommendations for Action
        Local Level
        State Level
        National Level
        Local, State, and National Levels

177   Appendix I

177   Organizations Active in Early Childhood Education and Child Care

185   Appendix II

185   Printed Material and Other Sources of Information

195   Appendix III

195   Sample Health Forms

201   Appendix IV

201   The AASA Survey on Early Childhood Education

Introduction

"We are embarking on a social experiment of enormous significance. Never before have so many of our infants and young children been cared for outside of the home on a regular basis...Unfortunately, this experiment was unplanned. It is a side effect of the social revolution of our society that began in the 1960s and changed our attitudes and values toward minorities, women, sex, marriage, family, and child rearing. Although we know why the experiment is being conducted, there is bitter disagreement as to *how* it is to be carried out."

—David Elkind, professor of child study and resident scholar at the Lincoln Filene Center for Citizenship and Public Affairs, Tufts University[1]

Under growing pressure from parents, state legislatures, and the public at large, public schools today are grappling with issues surrounding the establishment and operation of early childhood and child care programs for young children. The issues are difficult ones. They involve concerns over child care and the perception of the preschool years as a period crucial to children's social and emotional development. They also reflect a keen interest in academic preparation, school success, and global competition.

The United States is the only developed country without a national child care policy. With growing numbers of parents—

especially mothers—entering the work force, and with the day care needs of millions of children of working parents largely neglected by governments and employers, the lack of affordable child care is quickly reaching crisis proportions. Lack of viable child care services for the children of working parents may, in fact, have more to do with why mothers and fathers are turning to the public schools to provide preschool services than the much-touted theory that parents want to foster earlier academic preparedness for their children. Nonetheless, the desire for more rigorous schooling to prepare children for higher standards in elementary and secondary school and for the marketplace of the 21st century remains the rationale for some preschool initiatives.

Yet there's another reason for interest in early childhood development programs. In a country in which 25 percent of children live in poverty, these programs are increasingly seen by educators and others as one way to reverse the cycle of failure that often accompanies poverty. Early childhood development programs also have been shown to save society countless dollars by intervening to prevent educational and social problems before they occur. "Most of the growth of a human brain and body is completed in the first five years of life," notes UNICEF's 1988 "State of the World's Children" report. "There is no second chance."

Given these data, many educators and policy makers have moved from asking *whether* early childhood programs should be available to investigating *what kinds* of programs should be offered and *under whose sponsorship* they should be provided. And in many cases, although early childhood programs continue to be categorized as either educational or child care in nature, the traditional lines dividing such programs are becoming increasingly blurred as providers seek to include both components in well-rounded programs.

THE QUESTIONS—THE CONCERNS

As politicians, corporations, foundations, and taxpayers look more closely at how America's 18.3 million preschool-age children are cared for and educated, the role of the public schools has become central to the debate. Today's public school officials are being faced with such complex questions as:
- Are existing preschool programs in the community meeting parents' needs? If not, should the schools play a role in filling the gaps?
- Should schools offer new programs, expand current school-based programs (extend the kindergarten day, for example), or supplement existing community programs (work with child care centers

to ensure that parents' full-workday child care needs are met)?
- How will school-based preschool programs fit into the K-12 format? Who will operate these programs?
- What qualifications and training will be required of preschool teachers and administrators? On what salary schedule will they be paid?
- What children will take part in the programs (low-income, handicapped, at-risk, those with limited or no English proficiency, all children)?
- How will the program be funded (federal, state, local funds; parent fees; corporate sponsorship)?
- For how long will the program day run (half school day, full school day, full working day)?
- What will the program's philosophy be? How will it be articulated?
- Should a school-based program be academic in nature or should it follow child care models, stressing children's developmental needs?
- What about format, structure, curriculum, class size, adult-child ratios?
- What roles will reading, computers, and health care play?
- How will students be assessed? Will there be rules governing eligibility, screening, testing for readiness?
- How will the program involve parents? How will it address family needs, especially those of families in poverty?
- How will the program be evaluated?

SOME ANSWERS

Early Childhood Education and Child Care: Challenges and Opportunities for America's Public Schools provides some responses to these questions. It is designed to help schools and school communities that are creating or improving early childhood programs consider a number of important issues from many sides. In addition to reviewing the research and the current state of early childhood programs in the United States and elsewhere, this book gives direction on how to establish and maintain a successful program tailored to meet the specific needs of a community. Also included are many examples of successful early childhood program efforts and advice from experts and those in the trenches. Finally, the book concludes with a list of recommendations for action at the local, state, and federal levels—for the future of early childhood development and for the future of the nation.

In recent surveys conducted by the American Association of School Administrators asking administrators to identify issues of high importance and impact to the public schools, early childhood development and education were clearly growing concerns. No issues have risen so dramatically toward the top of the American agenda. Indeed, there are many challenges and opportunities for all those concerned about children. The care and education that our children are given today translates directly into the kind of society our country will have tomorrow.

---

1. David Elkind, "A Social Experiment of Enormous Significance," *Young Children*, November 1986, p. 2.

1

The Background, the Research, the Debate

"The future of our nation depends on the strength of its young people. We know that a majority of children will spend a significant part of their early years in child care settings. We must make certain that these settings provide all children with the support essential to their growth and development. We can do no less for these children, nor for the future health, strength, and economic competitiveness of our country."
—Children's Defense Fund[1]

Early childhood education and child care are indeed major issues of the 1980s. And they will most certainly continue to top national, state, and local agendas well into the 1990s. But why? What is happening across the nation that is causing such concern for our young children?

THE DEMOGRAPHIC PICTURE

The overwhelming interest in early childhood education and child care can be traced to a number of demographic factors. Among the most prominent are increases in the number of working mothers, rises in the number of children, changes in families, and poverty.

Working Women and Their Children

Consider, first, the statistics related to women in the workforce:
- More than 8.2 million mothers work outside the home, reports the Bureau of Labor Statistics; 200,000 more mothers join the labor force yearly.
- In 1940, 8.6 percent of mothers with children under 18 were in the labor force; by 1986, that number had risen to 63 percent. Also in 1986, 60 percent of mothers whose youngest child was three to five years old were employed—up from 45 percent 10 years earlier. And in 1986, 51 percent of mothers with children under age three were employed, up from 35 percent in 1976.
- In 1987, the share of new mothers who returned to work within a year of giving birth topped 50 percent for the first time. According to a U.S. Census Bureau report, dual-earner couples with children make up more than 40 percent of all married couples in the childbearing ages.
- By 1995, the Census Bureau predicts, 73 percent of all children under 18 will have mothers working outside the home, and that number will rise to 80 percent for children under age six. The U.S. House Select Committee on Children, Youth, and Families estimates that in 1990, 12.2 million children under age six will have working mothers.

There also has been a substantial increase in the preschool population after a decade of declining birth rates. According to Ellen Galinsky, director of Work and Family Life Studies at Bank Street College of Education and president of the National Association for the Education of Young Children, the number of children under age six has risen during the 1980s from 19.6 million to 21.2 million. By 1990, the number of children under age six is expected to reach 23 million, a 17.2-percent increase in just one decade.

Changes in the Family

Today's families have also changed. They tend to be smaller, move more frequently, and live farther away from relatives. The result: fewer opportunities for child care within families, neighborhoods, and communities. "We have moved from family care based primarily on the personal ties of kinship and neighborhood to care provided through specialized, impersonal, professional services," notes Urie Bronfenbrenner, Jacob Gould Schurman Professor of Human Development and Family Studies and of Psychology at Cornell University.[2]

The very nature of the family has also changed drastically.
- Currently, more than 20 percent of all births are to unmarried mothers, reports Family Service America (FSA), a national family

EARLY CHILDHOOD EDUCATION HAS HISTORICAL ROOTS

The idea of children starting school before age five is not new. The Puritans were concerned that children should learn to read the Bible as soon as possible, so they were often taught to read at age three or four. In 1647, Massachusetts enacted a law requiring that towns establish schools for young children. By the beginning of the 19th century, most Massachusetts towns offered schooling to the young. In 1826, 5 percent of all children enrolled in these schools were below the age of five.

At about this time the infant school, developed in Britain by Robert Owen, was introduced into the United States. These schools enrolled children as young as 18 months and were more activity-oriented than the primary schools. Many parents felt that their children could be taught more effectively in infant schools than at home in primary schools.

During the 1830s, the infant school movement faded. There was a sharp reduction in the enrollment of very young children in public schools because of an increased emphasis on children. Many voiced concern for balanced development, fearing that excessive intellectual activity in young children would cause insanity. In addition, schools were encouraged to exclude children less than six years old for bureaucratic reasons and to save money.

Kindergarten was introduced in the latter half of the 19th century as a more humane approach to educating young children. Also, kindergartens were more closely related to the family than either the early primary schools or infant schools.

SOURCE: Bernard Spodek, "Early Childhood Education's Past as Prologue: Roots of Contemporary Concerns," *Young Children*, July 1985.

organization. In fact, the traditional stereotype of the American family—working husband, housewife mother, and two school-age children—is no longer typical. In fact, it comprised less than 7 percent of U.S. households in 1985.
- In 1985, 11.7 percent of all households were maintained by a woman with no husband present, up from 8.7 percent in 1970.

- In 1984, 20 percent of white children under 18 and 59 percent of black children under 18 lived in single-parent families, compared with respective 1970 figures of 10 percent and 36 percent, according to FSA.
- Divorced persons now represent 9 percent of the U.S. population, up from 4 percent in 1970.

Children in Poverty

Poverty has also affected families—and children. Some 25 percent of America's children live in poverty, many of them in single-parent families headed by unemployed women. Childhood poverty often goes hand in hand with school failure, which in turn can lead to such problems as teenage pregnancy, drug and alcohol abuse, crime, and poverty in adulthood. Professor Bronfenbrenner calls poverty "the most rapid, the most recent, and the most consequential change" in American families.

The key to lifting children out of poverty is to move their parents out of poverty. But when federal and state funds and social programs for the poor are cut, families find it increasingly difficult to pull themselves out of poverty permanently, notes Robert Halpern of Columbia University's National Resource Center for Children in Poverty. In addition, the ability of young, low-income families to seek and obtain the jobs that might eventually remove them from the ranks of poverty is partly related to the availability of affordable child care, Halpern says, pointing to a significant and growing shortage of subsidized care for young low-income families.

The result is a gap in the quality of early childhood experiences between children living in poverty and those from better-off families. A two-tier system exists that allows the more well-to-do to purchase high-quality care and the less fortunate (including many middle-class children and those from working families) to receive marginal or inadequate care. Fifty-two percent of children in families with incomes of more than $20,000 take part in preschool programs, while only 29 percent of children in families with incomes of less than $10,000 participate in them, according to High/Scope, a research institute in Ypsilanti, Michigan (see Appendix I).

THE RESEARCH

America's interest in preschool programs has produced a growing body of research that reveals both benefits of and concerns about early childhood education.

The Benefits

Although most of the existing research concerns children at risk of school failure, some researchers have extrapolated the benefits of preschool to the entire population of children as a whole. Generally, high quality early childhood programs:
- Provide an environment that is safe and caring.
- Offer opportunities for children to learn.
- Strengthen families.
- Promote good health and nutritional practices.
- Prepare children for later school years.
- Help foster children's social, physical, emotional, cognitive, and psychological development.

One of the most frequently cited research bases for preschool programs is the Perry Preschool Project, conducted over the last 23 years by High/Scope. This was the first major longitudinal study to measure the effects of preschool education on the lives of children, and its results were clear: Disadvantaged children who have taken part in high quality preschool programs perform significantly better than those who have not. Participation in good preschool programs, the High/Scope researchers reported in "Changed Lives: The Effects of the Perry Preschool Project on Youths Through Age 19," helps lessen the risk of later failure in school and in life as a whole.

At-risk children who take part in good preschool programs:
- Maintain IQ gains for up to four years after the program has ended.
- Are assigned with less frequency to special education classes.
- Are held back in class less frequently.
- Are more likely to graduate from high school and pursue post-secondary education or training than those who do not take part in these programs.

A boon to parents and to society

The Perry study, which was released in 1984, also documented the benefit of good early education programs to parents and families as a whole. Mothers who participated in the Perry study increased their earning power due to expanded opportunities to participate in training and employment. Correspondingly, these mothers and their families had to rely less on social and welfare services than their non-participating counterparts.

Long-term benefits for at-risk students

Because good preschool programs reduce costs for special education, welfare, and the criminal justice system, the Perry study concluded that for every dollar invested in high quality programs

STUDIES BOLSTER PERRY FINDINGS

A number of research studies correlate the findings of the High/Scope Educational Research Foundation's Perry Preschool Project, including:

• The **Abecedarian Project**, an ongoing study of low-income children begun in the early 1970s by the Frank Porter Graham Child Development Center at the University of North Carolina at Chapel Hill, found that children who took part in high quality early childhood programs performed at a higher intellectual capacity during their initial primary school years than children who did not. The children also showed short-term gains on tests of cognitive ability and had fewer in-grade retentions.

• The **National Day Care Study**, the federal report released in 1979 by Abt Associates analyzing children from all income groups in licensed child care centers, also found increased short-term cognitive gains, as well as gains in social and emotional competence. Children who attended early childhood programs, the study found, were more responsible and talkative, initiated more social activities, and displayed more interest in classroom activities.

• The **Consortium for Longitudinal Studies**, a group of independent researchers who had conducted studies on the efficacy of early childhood programs in the 1960s, concluded that children who take part in preschool programs increase their IQ scores significantly, an effect that remains for three or four years. These children also perform better on reading achievement tests through the third grade and math tests through the fifth grade; are less likely to be placed in special education classes; are more likely to be promoted with their class and earn a high school diploma; and have higher occupational aspirations and expectations.

for at-risk children, seven dollars are returned to society in terms of savings on retention and remediation programs, lower dropout rates, and so forth. (The Committee for Economic Development's 1987 report, "Children in Need," places the savings at $4.75 for every dollar spent on early intervention programs, noting that, "The price of action may seem high, but the costs of inaction are far higher.")

"Early childhood is a time of life when, at least for some, the stream of poverty and scholastic failure can be diverted to a more successful course," writes Lawrence J. Schweinhart, director of High/Scope's Voices for Children project.[3] Indeed, early childhood programs' role in boosting children's development and helping break the cycle of poverty and failure has drawn policy makers and legislators to view public investment in such programs as worthwhile.

This type of evidence contributed to the establishment of a prekindergarten program for urban children in New Jersey, where an estimated 46,000 3- and 4-year-olds come from families who live below the federal poverty level of $11,200 annual income for a family of four. Coordinated by the New Jersey State Department of Education and the New Jersey State Department of Human Services, the program will cost about $10 million annually and is expected to enroll 1,150 3-year-olds and 1,150 4-year-olds in five or six districts. Participation in the program is voluntary and is offered at no cost to parents. Included are comprehensive educational, social, and health services, and parental involvement is encouraged. Among expected outcomes are:
- Better kindergarten preparation.
- Higher academic achievement rates in later grades.
- Better attendance.
- Higher self-confidence in academic and social skills.
- Greater student interest in school work.
- More parental involvement and support.

Reviews of the research on early childhood programs support the findings of the Perry Preschool study and introduce others. A 1985 review of Head Start research, for example, reiterated the cognitive gains and pointed to additional social and emotional benefits. CSR Incorporated found that children who attended high quality programs rated themselves more competent in school, were more responsible, and initiated more social activities. In addition, their greater access to health and dental care resulted in improved physical health and nutritional practices. The review also pointed to parents' improved access to educational, health, and social service systems.

The effect on bonding

Research has also served to allay parents' fears about potential negative effects of early separation from mothers. In fact, children

SUPPORT FOR EARLY CHILDHOOD PROGRAMS TARGETED FOR AT-RISK CHILDREN

A variety of individuals and groups, from businesspeople and educators to governors and mayors, have climbed on the bandwagon to endorse early childhood development programs for at-risk children. Consider these examples:

- The **Committee for Economic Development,** in its 1987 report, "Children in Need: Investment Strategies for the Educationally Disadvantaged," recommended high quality preschool programs for all disadvantaged 3- and 4-year-olds, as well as for the children of teenagers attending school. "By denying them the opportunity to learn and grow, we will not only be condemning these children individually but committing a terrible economic and social blunder as well," the report noted.
- The **National Governors' Association,** in its 1986 report, "Time for Results: The Governors' 1991 Report on Education," urged states to provide high quality early education for at-risk 4-year-olds and, where possible, for 3-year-olds. "Early childhood education has been offered as a powerful solution to student learning difficulties and for major dilemmas facing our society: crime, high dropout rates, welfare, and waste of human potential," noted one NGA document.
- **President George Bush,** in the budget he submitted to Congress in early 1989, proposed that low-income families receive a $1,000 tax credit or cash for the cost of caring for children up to four years old.
- In 1985, **Mayor Edward Koch,** announcing an initiative to provide early childhood education for all 4-year-olds in New York City, said he was "struck by the near unanimity among experts that, of all the educational and social programs initiated in the last 20 years, (early childhood education) is one that holds more promise than any other, an intervention on which there is solid and compelling research indicating its measurable and long-term positive effects on children's success in school and in life."

in high quality preschool programs appear to experience no significant disruption in maternal attachment. These children can develop just as well as those who stay at home with their mothers; and for children from low-income families, an early childhood program may offer enrichment that is not found at home.

The roots of early childhood education research

Finally, as we consider the wealth of recent research on early childhood programs, it is worth acknowledging an earlier current pointing toward the benefits of preschool programs. In the 1950s, for example, the work of Jean Piaget contributed enormously to a greater understanding of children's development. Researchers such as Benjamin Bloom, Burton White, Jerome Bruner, and J. McVicker Hunt in the 1960s disproved the doctrine of fixed intelligence that had guided educators and others in policy and program planning for many years before that.

Nonetheless, although the data available on the benefits of high quality preschool programs are overwhelmingly positive, certain caveats must be addressed.

The Concerns

Some gains may not be sustained

Among preschool programs' benefits, the intellectual and cognitive gains made by preschoolers raise the most controversy. Although most accept that these gains take place initially, some question whether they are maintained over time.

A three-year study of Head Start released in 1985, for example, concluded that while participants "enjoy significant immediate gains in cognitive test scores, socioemotional test scores, and health status," cognitive and socioemotional scores "do not remain superior to those of disadvantaged children who did not attend Head Start."[4] Others in the field echo this concern, noting that while most early childhood programs produce short-term benefits, quality is key to long-term success.

"Early childhood education should...help the graduates of preschool programs do better in school," notes Samuel G. Sava, the executive director of the National Association of Elementary School Principals. "The evidence is mixed on this: Typically, cognitive gains registered by preschoolers disappear a year or two after they enter first grade—but they do register those gains. The problem here is that we have not yet learned to adjust the 'fit' between preschool and the primary school curriculum to sustain the initial gains. In comparison with other aspects of schooling, early childhood education—as distinct from purely custodial child care—is still in its infancy, and we have a lot to learn from it."[5]

Research may not apply to all

Another research-related caution concerns the issue of generalization. Because the vast majority of research has focused on programs for disadvantaged and at-risk children, applying these studies' findings to all children may be wrong. In fact, most of the data available on middle-class children reveal that high quality early childhood programs have neither adverse nor beneficial effects. "Middle- and low-income children do not derive equal benefits from early intervention, and the greater benefits measured for low-income children cannot be generalized to the population as a whole," according to Sharon Lynn Kagan, director of the Office of Early Childhood Education in New York City and assistant professor of education at Yale University's Child Study Center.

Research in atypical settings

It is also important to recognize that much of the research has taken place in atypical settings such as universities, laboratory schools, and well-funded demonstration sites. "Compared with other preschool programs, the study programs are usually better funded, offer more comprehensive services, are more closely monitored, serve smaller groups of children, enroll fewer children per adult, and have especially well-trained staffs," Kagan notes. "The question remains as to whether the same high results can be achieved in less favored settings."[6]

Also clouding the research picture are the measures used to evaluate program effectiveness, a problem common to almost all research. Such measures, some say, are limited because they may be of questionable validity and may evaluate inappropriate outcomes.

No panacea

Finally, in light of positive research findings, experts and educators alike caution against viewing early childhood programs as the solution to schooling problems, poverty, and other societal ills. "Preschool education is a necessary, but not sufficient element of a response," says Columbia's Halpern, pointing to concerns that more will be expected of preschool education as a strategy to alleviate poverty than is reasonable to expect of any one response to a complex problem.[7]

The Committee for Economic Development, in its 1987 report, "Children in Need," noted that, "The nation's public schools have traditionally offered a common pathway out of poverty and a roadway to the American Dream." But, the CED cautioned that, "Today, in too many communities, the schools are ill-equipped to deal with the many needs of disadvantaged children. We believe that reform strategies for the educationally disadvantaged that focus on the school system alone will continue to fail these 'children in need.'" Instead, the group suggests strategies that include, but also go beyond, schools.

THE DEBATE

Support for prekindergarten programs is widespread. It is tied to evidence that such programs may help ease child care gaps that have reached crisis proportions and threaten to create a *de facto* two-tier system benefitting only those who can afford to pay for services. Endorsement also comes from those who believe that preschool programs for disadvantaged children help break the vicious cycle of poverty and failure. And support comes from those who see preschool programs as providing children the preparation necessary for the worldwide economic realities of the 21st century.

But not everyone supports every aspect of early childhood education. Some feel child care is the concern of parents only and shouldn't add to already overburdened school systems or non-parent taxpayers. Others voice concerns about who will provide the facilities and management for these programs, and who should be responsible for paying for them.

Central to the debate over early childhood programs are public school officials who have joined, and in some cases been forced into, the discussion. They find themselves center stage in part because of schools' unique role as the only major social institution that offers services to all children. They are there, too, because of a historical tendency to turn to the nation's public schools to address society's ills. Willing or not, schools are and will continue to be a central factor in the discussion as national organizations, politicians, parents, and others endorse early childhood programs in general and school-based programs in particular.

The Debate Over Sponsorship

Educators and public officials used to debate whether early childhood programs should be provided. Today, they are more likely to discuss the issue of sponsorship: What types of programs should be offered, who should provide them, and who will pay? The questions that guide this discussion and the answers they generate, practically everyone agrees, will shape the future of early childhood programs.

Early childhood and child care programs have for many years been publicly funded and community based. The sponsors have been social-service and health agencies, churches and synagogues, family day care homes, private and nonprofit programs, and, to a certain extent, corporations. Today, however, parents and policy makers are turning to the public schools, long the caretakers of children ages five and up, to assume more responsibility in the care of preschool-age children.

The issue of sponsorship—and who will control the funding and serve as the primary provider of early childhood programs—makes for bitter competition and threatens to erode efforts to provide the best programs for children. "The greatest impediment to the growth of early childhood programs is 'turf guarding,'" notes High/Scope's Schweinhart.

Turf guarding

Turf guarding takes place within local communities, where child care centers that have operated for years may view the public schools as "the new kid on the block." Among their concerns are that:
- Schools' traditional focus on academics works to the exclusion of developmental appropriateness.
- Teacher-student ratios are too high.
- Schools often neglect the needs of families, including working parents.
- Schools do not involve parents adequately.
- Schools can fail to meet the needs of minority preschoolers as they have done with minority school-age children in the past.

Competition and turf guarding also take place among state agencies responsible for administering funds. Often, these agencies have different philosophies, with social service departments seeking family and welfare support and education departments viewing programs as extensions of the K-12 program. Convinced of the importance of their mission, individuals within departments may fight to retain authority over specific programs. The result is lack of coordination of services and confusion among those attempting to obtain funding for programs.

Public schools as sponsors

Exacerbating these tensions is a growing public interest in public schools as sponsors of early childhood and child care programs. More than 3,000 of the nation's 15,000 school districts offer some type of early childhood education program today, according to current estimates. And legislators, fueled by research on the value of early intervention, have begun to allocate more funds to schools and away from state and local agencies that have traditionally provided these types of programs.

Support for public school sponsorship also can be traced to public schools' proven track record, as well as the trust most schools inspire among parents and public officials. Certification standards and salary schedules help ensure a high degree of professionalism among public school teachers—even if these standards and schedules don't necessarily apply to all school-based early childhood programs. And schools' access to public funds represents to many a less costly answer to increasing the availability of affordable child care.

The need for more programs

Availability is also a reason many are turning to the public schools. The stark reality is that there are not enough preschool programs to serve children, especially those at risk. In 1983, 53 percent of upper- and middle-income families enrolled their children in preschool programs, but only 29 percent of at-risk 3- and 4-year-olds took part in such programs, according to Ernest L. Boyer, president of the Carnegie Foundation for the Advancement of Teaching.

High/Scope describes the gap in programs this way: In 1983, only 424,000 poor 3- and 4-year-olds were enrolled in preschool child development programs, and not all the programs were of the quality needed to produce the long-term benefits described by the research. The National Governors' Association points out that existing child-care centers serve only 1.5 million of the 9 million preschool-age children whose mothers work. And a U.S. Government Accounting Office report notes that 60 percent of Aid to Families with Dependent Children work program respondents said lack of child care prevented program participation.

The concern that affluent families will be able to enroll their children in preschool programs and poor families will not has also spurred attempts to engage the public schools—with their commitment to providing education for all—in the care of prekindergarten-age children.

Getting children on the right track

Educators, in turn, often see the establishment of early childhood programs as a logical extension of their work. Mary Hatwood Futrell, former president of the National Education Association, supports the concept of lifelong learning. It is from this perspective that she backs preschool curriculums that "begin to help [children] develop the skills necessary for successful learning" and ease their transition to school. Indeed, administrators of successful early childhood programs point out that such programs start children on a success track and reduce the need for costly special education and remediation later in life. "Preschool programs, especially for at-risk children, have proven to be highly beneficial," notes Judy Spiegel, director of special programs for the **Milford, Delaware, School District**.

Administrators responding to a 1988 American Association of School Administrators survey conducted for this book cited research, working and single-parent families, and academic readiness as the rationale behind their districts' preschool programs.
- "Early intervention is key to positive and successful experiences in later school years," noted Ann Foster, language arts and early childhood specialist in the **Fort Collins, Colorado, School District**.
- Ruth Summerlin, kindergarten administrator for the **Savannah-Chatham Schools** in **Georgia**, pointed out that "review of research shows early intervention is required."
- And Ray Artz, elementary principal in the **Lena, Wisconsin, Public School District**, explained that "a significant number of children come to school from educationally deprived familial surroundings. Age six may be too late to make any noticeable change for those children."

Making optimum use of classrooms

In addition, as schools lose enrollment in the higher grades and the number of preschoolers rises, officials view preschool education as an attractive way to fill empty classrooms. Providing early childhood and child care services is also seen as wise because it can increase community and political support for the schools.

Challenges to School Responsibility

Of course, not everyone supports the concept of school-based early childhood and child care programs. The National Black Child Development Institute, for example, cautions against public school sponsorship based on the contention that the schools have yet to develop the skills and techniques necessary to nurture black talent "at its most fragile and formative stage..."

> The report card of public schools' treatment of black children is poor....All things being equal, if funding patterns of other urban public school programs for which minorities are the primary users apply, there is ample reason for concern that support for public school-based preschool programs would be inadequate in majority-black schools.

In its report, "Child Care in the Public Schools: Incubator for Inequality?," the NBCDI calls for careful study into the role the public schools would play in sponsoring early childhood programs. Until such issues as public school control of programs; changes in curriculum, staffing, and training; the schools' track record in addressing the needs of diverse populations; and the realism and willingness of the schools to address bias are examined, the Institute remains unable to support "wholesale proposals for public school child care." Without examining more closely the trend toward public school sponsorship, "Who...can assure us that we are not consigning our black babies to what may turn out to be nothing more than diaper ghettoes?" the group asks.[8]

Educators themselves also have expressed concern about public schools' role in providing early childhood programs. Asked whether they thought their school system was doing enough to provide early childhood education, a significant number of administrators who responded to the AASA survey said preschool was not a school responsibility. Among the comments:
- "We are educators—not family or child care agencies," said an assistant superintendent in South Carolina.
- "We offer kindergarten; anything prior to that is just a high-cost babysitting program," said an Iowa administrator.
- "We are moving toward the Soviet system of providing day care at any age," responded a Connecticut superintendent.
- And from a Montana superintendent, a recognition of tradition: "The scope of school financing and the history of school functions has been on teaching rather than custodial functions."

Even among administrators who support the concept of school-based early childhood programs, some say a lack of funds keeps them from offering such programs. "How can I think about an early childhood education program when proper financial support for the present school program is inadequate?" asked an Ohio superintendent.

However, simply making those funds available to public schools does not mean that child care services would be provided. In a 1988 survey conducted by the National Association of Elementary School Principals, K-8 principals were asked whether they would provide child care for school-aged children if provided with adequate resources. Almost 26 percent of the respondents said they would not.

Counterpoints

NAESP Executive Director Sava has responded by pointing out that the public schools are the most appropriate place for early childhood programs. The reason: Schools are the only major social institution set up to provide full services to children. While agreeing that financial constraints keep many schools from embracing early childhood programs, Sava nonetheless points out, "There is no doubt in my mind that the schools will be involved, because it's politically and socially driven." School officials, if they are truly advocates for children, he says, "have no choice" but to provide programs *and* to fight for funding at the local, state, and federal levels. "Superintendents might want to hold back, but I think that's a mistake," he adds. "The role of the school is to educate children, and there is a desperate need for quality early childhood education."

High/Scope's Schweinhart concurs. The real issue, he says, is not whether early childhood programs are the public schools' responsibility, but what kinds of services must be provided and who should provide them. The bottom line for administrators, according to Schweinhart, is, "If not you, who?"

Enrollment trends

Enrollment figures also point to increased interest in preschool programs in schools:
- In the last decade, the enrollment rate for 3- and 4-year-olds has almost doubled, notes High/Scope, rising from 21 percent of that population in 1970 to 38 percent in 1983. Rates for 5-year-olds also increased, climbing from 78 percent in 1970 to 93 percent in 1983.
- According to the 1983 census, 2.6 million 3- and 4-year-olds—or 37.6 percent of that population—were enrolled in preprimary school.
- Enrollment levels in independent school preschool programs are also on the rise. The National Association of Independent Schools, with 940 member schools, reported a 43-percent increase from 1981-82 to 1987-88 in the number of students in prekindergarten programs.

Economic support

Public interest in child care can also be illustrated economically. Consider the following expenditures for prekindergarten programs:
- In 1986, 22 states and the District of Columbia spent $330 million to fund early childhood programs; by 1987, 6 more states had joined the ranks of those providing preschool programs. Compare this to the $160 million appropriated by only 8 states in 1984, and it is not difficult to see how far interest in such programs has come. (It should be noted that these state-funded programs are designed, for the most part, to serve at-risk children: those who live in poverty, those who are handicapped, and those for whom English is a second language.)
- Between 1984 and 1989, 48 states passed more than 350 pieces of legislation in response, in part, to a lack of federal child care legislation, according to the National Conference of State Legislatures.
- In addition, 28 of the largest urban school districts appropriated

$136 million in 1985-86 to fund prekindergarten programs for approximately 70,000 children, according to High/Scope.

It is these indicators that prompted Sava to proclaim at the 1986 annual meeting of the National Association for the Education of Young Children: "The burgeoning American acceptance of early childhood education is clearly no fad, no trendy 'innovation' that will wither for lack of sustained social and parental interest after a few years of enthusiasm; constant enrollment increases demonstrate that."

Ensuring Quality

In addition to legislative and public support for prekindergarten programs, there have been a number of recent efforts to encourage further debate of early education issues and to help ensure that programs that are established are of high quality. Among them:

- The **American Association of School Administrators** adopted a policy statement for dealing with child care issues facing the 101st Congress. Among the planks of the statement: There should be an increase in child care/early childhood education programs and services for children age five and under. These programs must be of high quality and developmentally appropriate. There should be inter-agency collaboration and cooperation to support the provision of comprehensive family services among school, state, and community agencies. The federal government must fund whatever legislation is passed.
- The **Council of Chief State School Officers** has called on states to guarantee high quality programs and services for at-risk children. "There is no more essential or more sensitive challenge before us than to create new partnerships and shared responsibilities for the development of young children," the group noted in an official statement. Among CSSO's recommendations were universally available high quality early childhood services for all children, especially those at risk; programs for new parents; developmentally appropriate preschool education and day care programs; and collaboration among public and private groups in providing health, social, and educational services to young children and their families.
- The **National Association of State Boards of Education,** with a two-year, $300,000 grant from the Carnegie Corporation, chose four states to assist in charting early childhood development policy. In Alaska, Delaware, Oregon, and Virginia, the NASBE is working toward making state boards of education the facilitators of early childhood policy, bringing together representatives from Head Start and the child care community to design

standards and train teachers. To further explore the issues, the NASBE appointed a representative Early Childhood Education Task Force, which held public hearings with parents, teachers, administrators, and education policy makers in the four states. The panel also visited 16 public and private school sites and reviewed commissioned papers and presentations of leading experts in the field. In its 1988 report, "Right from the Start," the group stressed the importance of positive early school experiences in developing attitudes that foster learning. It also recommended that elementary schools establish early childhood units to provide a new pedagogy for working with 4- through 8-year-olds, as well as a focal point for enhanced services for preschoolers and their parents.

- The **National Conference of State Legislatures**, which in 1985 declared that early childhood education and child care were "the most significant new areas of legislative activity in education," works with state legislatures to develop prekindergarten policy.
- The **Association for Supervision and Curriculum Development** is also committing more of its energies to early childhood education, based on what ASCD Executive Director Gordon Cawelti calls "the compelling research." In addition to conferences and publications, the group has developed an official ASCD network in early childhood education designed to foster discussion of the issues.
- The **American Federation of Teachers** has since the 1970s supported public-school sponsorship of early childhood programs.
- The **National Education Association,** which also supports early childhood programs, is looking into the feasibility of establishing neighborhood day care as an adjunct to public education.
- The **Alliance for Better Child Care**, a coalition of some 70 national organizations, joined in 1987 to create national child care policy and promote federal legislation.
- **Bank Street College of Education** and the **Wellesley College Center for Research on Women** in 1988 completed a study of public school involvement in early childhood programs. Bank Street is also looking at how prekindergarten programs are funded and set up nationwide.
- The **Carnegie Foundation for the Advancement of Teaching**, through its "Early Years" project, will examine educational and child care programs for children from birth to age eight.
- Based on increased interest in preschool programs and calls for quality, the **National Association for the Education of Young Children** has developed the country's only national,

voluntary accrediting system for early childhood and child care programs.
- The **National Association of Elementary School Principals** is working to develop requirements for elementary school teachers and principals who work with preschoolers. The NAESP and the High/Scope Educational Research Foundation have provided training sessions for principals. They also have published "A Principal's Guide to Early Childhood Programs," a guide for elementary administrators.
- Concerned that public school sponsorship of early childhood programs may be harmful to black children, the **National Black Child Development Institute** published a policy paper on issues key to the development of high quality programs.

A Growing Necessity

Child care issues have long been closely tied to a broader debate about the role of government in family life. Today, Columbia University's Halpern points out, "Reality has made the debate irrelevant because the great majority of low- and moderate-income mothers of young children now have to work to keep their family

---

AASA POSITION STATEMENT ON EARLY CHILDHOOD EDUCATION

AASA supports policies that will make it possible for all children, including those who are disadvantaged, to receive the services of their schools at an early age. An increasing number of children, ages three to five, could benefit from school-based child development activities that will enhance their abilities to socialize and later become even more successful in school and in life. When possible, those programs should be designed to assist parents in increasing their parenting skills. Early childhood education programs should be appropriate for individual children since research has shown that overly ambitious programs, aimed at students who are not ready, can begin a cycle of failure.

SOURCE: *Let's Discuss the Issues*, American Association of School Administrators, p. 7

above subsistence....We as a society face the urgent task of renewing and redefining our social contract with each other, and with young families in particular," he notes. "The early childhood care and education community has a central responsibility with respect to this task."[9]

Indeed, many of those who make up the early childhood education community have recognized this responsibility. "Like a barometer, early childhood programs respond to change in the social, political, and economic climates," according to Paula Jorde, assistant professor at the National College of Education. "But [they do] more than merely respond to societal changes, and may in fact serve as an important agent of change....In both responding to and initiating changes, early childhood education seems once again at the forefront of America's consciousness."[10]

Ronald Mcleod, superintendent of schools in **El Paso, Texas**, another advocate of early childhood education programs, addressed their effectiveness, especially with regard to at-risk children. "Early childhood education has a significant impact on later schooling, especially on economically deprived and limited-English-speaking students. We've seen that those students in the program have progressed at a much greater rate than those that have not had the early childhood education experience. Of course, there is the cost factor, but I really feel the payoff for later success is well worth the cost that is created in a district."

WHERE TO START

Those witnessing or involved in the current debate over sponsorship offer several suggestions for public schools debating their role. School officials who want to expand services to preschoolers, they say, should begin by offering programs for those low-income, handicapped, or English-as-a-second-language students whose parents want and need these services. In addition, schools would be wise to offer extended-day child care to fill the gap before and after traditional school hours and help working parents. Given today's demographics, part-day programs that fail to address working parents' child care needs make little sense, many advocates say.

Besides instituting programs of their own, schools can promote early childhood education in other ways. For example, schools—especially those that are financially strapped—might provide information and referral services to acquaint parents with child care options that exist in the community. Schools might also enter into partnerships with existing child care providers to expand the availability and lower the cost of child care.

Whatever school leaders decide, those that choose to offer programs should work with members of the child care field to provide programs that are best for children. Some state legislators, mindful of this advice, have worked to encourage cooperation and coordination among agencies dealing with children, especially those that deal with child care and early childhood education. They have mandated coordination of standards for licensing providers and the selection of one agency to administer all child care programs. They also have offered incentives to various providers to work together for the benefit of children.

To determine the different types of early childhood and child care programs available, let's turn now to a discussion of what early childhood programs are.

Notes

1. Children's Defense Fund, "Child Care: The Time Is Now" (Washington, D.C.: Children's Defense Fund, 1987), p. 3.
2. Urie Bronfenbrenner, "The Three Worlds of Childhood," *Principal*, May 1985, p. 8.
3. Lawrence J. Schweinhart, *The Preschool Challenge* (Ypsilanti, Mich.: High/Scope Educational Research Foundation, 1985), p. 8.
4. Ruth Hubbell McKey, et. al., "The Impact of Head Start on Children, Families, and Communities: Final Report of the Head Start Evaluation, Synthesis and Utilization Project" (Washington, D.C.: CSR, Incorporated, June 1985), p. 1.
5. Samuel G. Sava, "The Endangered Promise," foreword to *A School Administrator's Guide to Early Childhood Programs*, by Lawrence J. Schweinhart (Ypsilanti, Mich.: High/Scope Educational Research Foundation, 1988), p. vi.
6. Sharon L. Kagan, "4-Year-Olds and the Schools," *Education Week*, December 11, 1985, p. 24.
7. Robert Halpern, "Major Social and Demographic Trends Affecting Young Families: Implications for Early Childhood Care and Education," *Young Children*, September 1987, p. 38.
8. "Child Care in the Public Schools: Incubator for Inequality?" (Washington, D.C.:, National Black Child Development Institute, Inc., 1985) pp. 5, 18-19, 26.
9. Robert Halpern, p. 34.
10. Paula Jorde, "Early Childhood Education: Issues and Trends," *The Educational Forum*, Winter 1986, p. 171.

What Are Early Childhood Programs?

"In years past, the definition of [early childhood education] was a rather narrow one, referring to the planned educational experiences of young children ages three through five in group settings. Today, the term...is used to reflect a far more inclusive view of children and their educational experience. Some go so far as to say that early education includes virtually 'everything' that happens to the young child from birth through the initial years of formal schooling."
—Paula Jorde, assistant professor,
National College of Education[1]

The phenomenon of early childhood programs—what David Elkind has called "a social experiment of enormous significance" in which many of the country's children are cared for outside the home on a regular basis—is quickly moving beyond its initial stage into a permanent niche in American society.

Because of their role in addressing the country's lack of available and affordable child care, intervening in the lives of at-risk children, and preparing tomorrow's adults for the future, early childhood programs have captured the attention of a significant sector of the public, from welfare mothers to U.S. senators.

Despite their popularity, there is some confusion about what early childhood programs are. In the AASA survey of public school administrators conducted for this publication in 1988, for example,

respondents defined the scope of early childhood programs in a variety of ways:
- Most considered preschool/prekindergarten programs for 3- to 5-year-olds and kindergarten programs for 5-year-olds part of early childhood programs.
- Several included Head Start and the early elementary grades.
- Few considered before- and after-school care within the purview of early childhood programs.
- Almost no one considered infant/toddler programs part of the definition.
- Other areas mentioned by some respondents included transitional first grade, developmental kindergarten, programs for the handicapped, and parenting services.

Although there are almost as many definitions for early childhood programs as there are types of programs, there is general agreement that early childhood programs provide care and sometimes education to children from birth to ages six or eight. From family day care and nursery schools to child care centers and kindergarten programs, they may provide half- or full-day care, include outreach services to families, or focus on academic enrichment, among a number of other options.

In coming to terms with definitions of early childhood programs, it should be noted that preschool programs with an "educational" component and child care are not necessarily mutually exclusive. All education programs for children under six involve child care and nurturing, and most child care programs include some form of education in the broadest sense of learning.

Also key to developing an understanding of early childhood programs is comprehending how programs are funded and regulated.

THE RANGE OF PROGRAMS

In an attempt to define various types of early childhood programs, it is helpful to consider sponsorship. Early childhood programs are offered by private and public groups on profit-making and nonprofit bases. They are funded by state and local taxes; they receive federal and parent support; and they are run by churches, social service centers, schools, and corporations, among others.

Another way to understand the varieties of early childhood programs is to look at their function. Programs are established to respond to working parents' child-care needs, to prepare children to enter kindergarten, to provide special services to infants or to English-as-a-second-language children, and to meet many other goals.

Keeping both sponsorship and function in mind, let's take a

look at the wide array of types of programs, many of which overlap with one another.

Self-Care

Self-care occurs when children take care of themselves unsupervised. Although self-care cannot be characterized as a program, it is how an estimated 7 million preschool children of working parents are cared for at various times during the day, according to the National Commission on Working Women.

Parents of young children who are left to take care of themselves—and sometimes younger siblings—are usually unable to find affordable child care or are afraid of losing their jobs if they stay home when their patchwork child care arrangements fall through from time to time.

The drawbacks to this type of care are obvious and include health and safety risks. Not as obvious are setbacks suffered by these children in terms of self-esteem, security, and learning abilities.

In-Home Care by Others

As many as 10 million children are cared for in their own homes, according to the NCWW. Many are cared for by relatives, neighbors, babysitters, and nannies who frequently are older women who lack formal child development training but may have raised children of their own. This type of care is beneficial because it allows children to remain in their own homes, which is often best for infants. It also may help parents by saving on transportation costs and time.

But there are drawbacks to in-home care. Children usually are not exposed to the wide variety of creative toys, materials, and structured activities available in child care centers and schools. They do not have the socialization opportunities that come from interacting with peers (other than siblings). And they may watch television more and interact less with caregivers than children in out-of-home care.

Family Day Care

Experts estimate that from a third to a half of all children under age five receive child care from a family day care provider. Family care is provided in the caretaker's home, and may be offered for all or part of the day. It generally includes from two to six children per adult, depending on the ages of the children and regulations.

Although family day care is usually provided by individuals, some providers form family day care networks to share responsibilities, expertise, and equipment. And though it is rare, public schools can also provide family day care. **Hayward Unified School District,** for example, runs a "satellite family day care" program providing daily care from 7 a.m. to 6 p.m. for 2- to 5-year-olds in five family day care homes. Caregivers contract with the district to provide services for five children in their homes. The program is supervised by a resource teacher and a child care supervisor from the district, and fees range from free to $12 daily, depending on family income.

Among the benefits of family day care: a setting similar to a home, mixed-age grouping of children, and a caretaker with a "motherly" manner who has probably had more training than a babysitter or other at-home caregiver.

The disadvantages of family day care programs are similar to those of care in the child's own home: They may lack the wide range of toys and materials in child care centers and schools, and they may not provide adequate opportunities for activities that promote growth and development. In addition, while there is some state and local regulation of family day care homes, it is estimated that only a fifth of these programs are licensed. Experts speculate there is a large number of "underground" family day care homes that are unregistered and therefore unmonitored.

Nursery Schools

Nursery schools enroll children aged two-and-a-half to five in half-day programs, usually two to five times per week. These programs often feature an educational component, and are often privately operated by individuals, proprietary companies, and religious organizations. Nursery school teachers often have had child development training at the college level.

Nursery schools' strong points include formats that allow organized activities geared to children's development, professional teachers, and opportunities to interact with other children.

Among their weak points: Their hours of operation often do not meet working parents' needs for child care, their focus may be too academic for some children and parents, and they can be more costly than child care programs or family day homes.

Child Care Centers

An estimated 1.5 million children under age five whose mothers work attend child care centers, according to the NCWW. Child or day care centers generally do not offer formal academic

Kindergarten

While preschool programs are often defined as prekindergarten programs, kindergarten represents public schools' earliest foray into pre-first-grade schooling. Designed for 5-year-olds (though some programs have begun to admit younger students), kindergartens usually feature one teacher and a room full of students learning numbers and letters, playing, and interacting with others. Eighty-five percent of American 5-year-olds took part in kindergarten programs in the 1980s, according to the National Center for Education Statistics, up considerably from the 5 percent of 5-year-olds who attended kindergarten in 1901.

Kindergarten attendance remains for the most part noncompulsory, but a growing number of states have considered making it compulsory or instituting a readiness test for admission to first grade.[3]

Trend toward full-day programs

In many states and districts where half-day programs are traditional, there has been a trend toward lengthening the program day—thus increasing the time available for activities. In 1985, 29 percent of kindergartens in the United States operated on full-day schedules.

Such programs are popular because they meet parents' child care needs and reduce schools' transportation costs by eliminating mid-day bus trips. But there is evidence that this trend is also due to academic considerations:

- Public officials say they provide more time for early intervention.
- More children are taking part in earlier schooling or child care experiences, making them ready, some say, for full-day schooling at age five.
- Longer days provide more opportunities for a varied curriculum, more time for individualized attention, and more chances to screen and assess.
- Researchers point to more short-term academic gains and higher test scores for full-day kindergarteners than for their counterparts in half-day programs.

In the AASA survey for this book, a quarter of the respondents said their schools offer full-day kindergartens. "We initiated a full-day program to lessen the pressure on students," explains Robert M. McGuire, superintendent of the **Northvale, New Jersey, public schools.** "Our curriculum was too tight and had eliminated much play and socialization."

The half-day, full-day debate

Opponents of full-day programs express concern that 5-year-olds are not physically and emotionally ready for the stress of full-day programs and that these programs may be too academic. They also point to added expenses needed to hire additional teachers and provide more space and equipment, costs that may not be offset by savings in transportation or other areas. Furthermore, they note, full-day participants' higher tests scores are not retained over time, leveling off in the early elementary grades.

Opponents also note that full-school-day programs may not meet parents' child care needs because they are almost always shorter than full working days. Lawrence J. Schweinhart, director of the Voices for Children project of the High/Scope Educational Research Foundation, advocates half-day kindergarten programs with supplemental child care to meet working parents' needs. Notes Schweinhart: "Full-school-day programs serve mainly bus drivers' schedules."

Proponents of half-day kindergarten programs, including many educators who have lived with this traditional model for years, say these programs provide high quality learning and socialization experiences for children while helping them make the appropriate transition to school. Such programs, they say, are less stressful, take into account 5-year-olds' attention span, and allow children to experience out-of-school settings at home or in child care.

For schools, half-day programs call for added transportation, but they also represent savings since they require fewer teachers and less space and equipment. Nearly three-quarters of the administrators responding to the AASA survey said their schools offer half-day programs.

Opponents of half-day programs cite the midday disruption of moving children from one setting to another and the difficulties parents encounter when neither transportation nor supplemental care is provided. They also note that much time is spent in start-up and wrap-up activities, and that children have less opportunity to take part in field trips and other time-consuming activities. [4]

Duration is just one important factor

While full- and half-day programs have their advantages and disadvantages, it is worth noting in any assessment of the kindergarten debate that the length of the school day is but one program issue. Early childhood experts stress the importance of considering not just *quantity* but *quality* in kindergarten programs. No matter what the length of day, kindergarten programs should have developmentally appropriate curriculums, consistent schedules, and qualified staff. They also must be carefully planned and consistently evaluated.

Furthermore, researchers suggest that group size is more important than length of day in the achievement of disadvantaged kindergarteners. And for some children, providing opportunities for different kinds of kindergarten—developmental or transitional—may be more important than lengthening or shortening the school day. (See related discussion in Chapter 3.)

Other Kindergarten Program Alternatives

Transitional programs

A number of districts have also begun to offer transitional or developmental programs. Based on research showing that not all children are ready to begin kindergarten at age five, these programs feature reduced class sizes and provide an "in-between" year emphasizing physical activity over pencil-and-paper work.

Former Secretary of Education William Bennett, in "First Lessons: A Report on Elementary Education in America," suggested "we may be better off building in a 'pre-first' grade transition year for some youngsters, and sending them to first grade when they are seven, rather than assuming that every child's greatest need is for organized, cognitive learning at five."

There is some debate over the value of these transitional or developmental kindergarten programs, however. Proponents support such programs' smaller class size and their emphasis on individualized attention and non-academic work, pointing out that many children are not ready for pencil-and-paper work at this age. But opponents view the placement of children of this age in transitional classes as tantamount to retaining them, a practice they consider not only costly but unsuccessful.

Programs for Handicapped Children

In the last 10 years, states have either made the delivery of educational services to all 3- to 5-year-old handicapped children a legal requirement or, more frequently, mandated services for some portion of that population. Many targeted programs enacted by state legislatures, some of which receive federal funds, have focused on providing early intervention to special-needs children. And the federal government, under the 1986 Education of the Handicapped Act amendments, PL 99-457, created a preschool early intervention and special education program.

In **Columbus, Ohio,** for example, the preschool program provides early educational experiences appropriate to handicapped children's level to help ameliorate the effects of the handicapping conditions. The program also strives to help students develop to their fullest potential, and provides parents with information and support along the way. Similarly, the **Burleson, Texas, Indepen-**

dent School District program works to increase eligible handicapped students' skills so they may be successful in the regular school program. The program enrolls 3- to 5-year-olds with handicapping conditions and children from birth to age five who are hearing or sight impaired. There is also a walk-in speech program.

The limited availability of programs

These and similar programs aside, special education experts remain concerned over the limited availability of preschool programs for handicapped children. In 1984-85, about 295,000 children under age five (88 percent of whom were between the ages of three and five) received special education and related services under PL 94-142 and the Preschool Incentive Grant Program, according to the U.S. Education Department's Office of Special Education and Rehabilitative Services. Yet it is estimated that more than half of the nation's handicapped 3- to 5-year-olds remain unserved; this number is higher for children under age three.

In addition, some children who take part in programs are underserved due to low funding, inadequate staff training, and the lack of research on how best to serve this population. There is also considerable variation from state to state in the ways children are screened and evaluated for enrollment in programs for the handicapped. The result is that the number of handicapped children identified to take part in preschool programs and the programs themselves vary significantly from state to state.

Programs for the Gifted and Talented

Because research indicates that a substantial amount of an individual's intellectual and creative ability is developed during early childhood, young children who are identified as gifted and talented should be given the opportunity to participate in an enriched learning environment, according to Gail E. Hanninen, gifted coordinator of the **Kalispell, Montana, School District.** Children who perform significantly above their age level in language development, thinking skills, creative thinking, physical adaptability, social skills, or leadership can be identified through state or local criteria and placed in appropriate programs, according to Hanninen. "Consequently, a child's readiness to learn and to create is the determining factor in the type of learning experiences presented," explains Hanninen. "Such an opportunity should take into consideration the fact that demonstrated advanced ability in one area may not necessarily mean similar levels of performance in all areas."[5]

Extended-Day Care

Extended-day child care, also known as before- and after-school care, is offered by public schools, community agencies, child care centers, family day care homes, and others to fill the child care gap left by partial-day programs. Some educators and child care experts point to extended-day programs as the next logical step for public schools interested in expanding their services to meet the needs of working parents. Others feel the schools are not the place for what they term "babysitting services." At least 10 states have passed legislation addressing the use of schools for before- and after-school child care, according to the National Conference of State Legislatures.

In a survey conducted by the National Association of Elementary School Principals in 1987-88, 84 percent of elementary and middle school principals said children in their communities need supervision before and after school. But only 22 percent said their schools offered such programs. Among the reasons: inadequate staff and funding, authority, and a reluctance among some to assume the added responsibility.

A significant number of respondents to the AASA survey agreed overwhelmingly that before- and after-school care is not a public school responsibility—but one that should be assumed by the family, churches and synagogues, the community, and private providers. For administrators in rural areas, the issue was less pressing than for those in urban and suburban regions, where children are more likely to return home after school to empty houses.

Among those administrators whose schools offer extended-day programs, after-school programs were much more prevalent than before-school options. There was a consensus that extended-day programs were low-priority items—often among the first to be cut from tight budgets, especially if the need was being met elsewhere in the community.

A shared responsibility

Responding to such comments, Fern Marx of the School-Age Child Care Project at the Wellesley College Center for Research on Women in Wellesley, Massachusetts, counters that, "The question isn't, 'Are they responsible?' but 'Are they part of the community?' It's a shared responsibility." This is so especially, she adds, in light of increasing agreement among teachers and others that one of the major factors contributing to learning problems among children is self-care, or inadequate before- and after-school care. Marx also notes that schools don't have to provide programs in this area, but should play a role as responsible community members, providing space for others to offer programs, encouraging local business support, and so forth.

One district that does provide programs is the **Hayward, California, Unified School District.** Its "Kids' Club" provides before- and after-school child care for children in kindergarten through third grade. Payment is based on a sliding-fee scale, and subsidized slots are available.

In **Murfreesboro, Tennessee,** the city school system recently celebrated the third anniversary of its Extended School Program. The project, which operates before- and after-school hours, aims to help students and staff get the most out of after-school hours. Youngsters can take music lessons, learn about computers, get a head start on homework, or attend Boy Scout or Girl Scout meetings, to name but a few options. Fees range from $10 to $25 per week per child; summer-session fees are approximately $40 per week. "As superintendent, I saw the resources available for school-age child care and the need for an extended school program being meshed to produce a meaningful, workable, and affordable experience for millions of children across America," says Superintendent John H. Jones.

Other Public School Programs

As indicated, public schools may offer many of the early childhood programs that have been described, from nursery schools and child care centers to infant and toddler care. They may work in conjunction with community agencies or offer programs independently. Programs may be targeted to a specific segment of the community or available to all students.

In **Florissant, Missouri,** the **Ferguson-Florissant School District** offers a Saturday School program designed to help all the district's 4-year-olds. Parents volunteer to assist teachers in morning or afternoon classes, and teachers visit homes to reinforce lessons. Home activity guides provide parents with follow-up learning activities for the week.

The Diego Elementary School, a unit of the **Chicago public schools,** serves minority students with a mixture of Head Start, bilingual education, and special education funds. And the Chicago schools' Dewey Child Parent Center, serving children from low-income families from three years old through kindergarten, operates out of a facility adjacent to an elementary school.

More and more, schools are sponsoring related programs—such as parent education. Although not considered child care or early schooling per se, parent education programs are designed to help parents understand the complexities of childrearing. And in many districts and states, for example, parent education programs go hand-in-hand with preschool programs. Missouri's nationally acclaimed "Parents as Teachers" program begins soon after childbirth. Other programs offer parents support and assistance, put them in touch with social service agencies, and encourage them to come together with other parents to discuss problems. (For more information on parent involvement and parent education programs, see Chapter 6.)

Employer-Sponsored Child Care

A growing number of employers have begun to offer child care services. Among their reasons: a recognition that working parents need affordable and available care and an awareness that providing these services reduces parents' anxiety over child care and improves employee performance (there is less absenteeism and tardiness, higher staff morale, and better concentration). According to Sandra Hamburg, Co-director of the Committee for Economic Development's Project on Education and Child Development, businesses "have come to realize that working parents cannot fully attend to their jobs." She believes that corporations hoping to recruit from the ever-increasing pool of women and single parents in the work force are finding that they must provide for the child care of their employees as a benefit.

Many businesses have begun to respond to this new trend in hiring practices. Similarly, in some parts of the country where unemployment is low, they find they must offer some form of child care (or adult care) benefit in order to attract workers. And greater numbers of policy makers are encouraging businesses to play a role in providing child care.

Today, about 3,000 businesses provide some type of child care benefit to their employees, more than four times the number that provided child care benefits in 1982. With 6 million businesses, though, the number represents but a drop in the bucket. In addition, most employer assistance takes the form of information and referral services rather than on-site care.

Corporate Child Care Services of **Nutley, New Jersey,** owned and operated by Hoffmann-LaRoche, Inc., is one of the 600. A fully developed on-site corporate child care program begun in 1977, the center is open to children from ages two and a half to eight. It provides full- and part-time care, after-school care, summer and drop-in care, emergency care, and a full-day kindergarten program available to employees at approximately $400 per month per child.

On-site programs for young children

Superintendent Joseph Fernandez, of the **Dade County, Florida, public schools,** also has developed an innovative relationship with area businesses that has proven mutually beneficial to all concerned. As a benefit to their employees, the American Banker's Insurance Group and the Miami International Airport, for example, now provide facilities for employees' 6-week-old to 2nd grade children. The public school system provides the teachers, the equipment, and the supplies, in exchange for the space, utilities, and security. So that children do not feel too insulated or are not deprived of benefits available in a larger school system, children of these satellite learning centers participate in school assemblies and other activities with students at a nearby "host" school. Executive Assistant to the Superintendent Joseph Tekerman noted that not only is it a great perk for the employees, "Now children know what mommy and daddy do when they go off (to work)."

Other alternatives for employers

Besides on-site care, employers may offer subsidies or vouchers that employees can redeem at area child care centers. They might also offer alternative work patterns such as job sharing and flex time to accommodate working parents' needs. States such as Connecticut, Oregon, and Rhode Island have passed legislation offering tax breaks to businesses that offer child care assistance, according to NCSL. At least 32 states provide or plan to provide some type of child care assistance to their state employees.

Another example of an innovative day care program benefits employees of the **Arlington, Virginia, public schools.** The Arlington School Employee's Children's School Center, which serves children between the ages of two months and five years, is funded through loans from the employee credit union. The center is open from 6:30 a.m. to 6:00 p.m., and is located in a central location in the district so that parents can visit their children during the day. School officials view the center as especially effective in recruiting and retaining good teachers and other staff, so the center benefits the entire school system.

FUNDING EARLY CHILDHOOD PROGRAMS

Key to understanding differences among early childhood programs is an understanding of how these programs are funded. This area has traditionally generated confusion—given the existence of dozens of funding sources, channels, and methods used in preschool programs, and the fact that programs often take advantage of a variety of each.

Obviously, quality is expensive. High/Scope's Perry Preschool study cost $5,000 per child per year in 1981 dollars, for example. And costs of operating early childhood programs vary depending on program content, hours of operation, qualifications and number of staff, type and number of children enrolled, location, support services provided, materials, transportation, and sponsorship.

Federal Funds

The federal government is the primary provider of public funds for preschool programs. Early childhood programs are funded in a wide variety of ways, with some options—such as Chapter 1, Head Start, and federal grants—more accessible to public schools than others. Federal support is provided through funds given to families, states, and local organizations, through federal income tax credits for families and businesses, and through tax deductions for program-supporting contributions.

In fiscal year 1987, the federal government spent $3.3 billion on preschool and child care programs, according to David Weikart, president of High/Scope. The breakdown was as follows:
- $1.1 billion to Project Head Start, which provides federal matching funds for programs to help improve the social and learning skills and the nutrition and health status of low-income children.
- $1.1 billion to the Title XX Social Services Block Grant, which provides federal funds to states for social services to be determined at the states' discretion.
- $373 million to the Child Care Food Program, which was authorized under the National School Lunch Act and which provides funds to reimburse participating child care centers and family and group day care homes for the cost of providing meals and snacks for children.
- $345 million to special education services.
- $298 million to compensatory education services.
- $35 million to Defense Department programs.
- $5 million to the Dependent Care Block Grant.

High/Scope also reports that some 63 percent of 3- and 4-year-olds, or about 4.4 million children, receive some federal assistance to participate in early childhood programs. Excluding the tax credit program, 25 percent of 3- and 4-year-olds—some 1.8 million children—are in early childhood education or care programs funded by federal grants.

Additional federal funds were spent in 1987 on the Child and Dependent Care Tax Credit, which provides indirect support in the form of an income tax credit primarily for those who work or are seeking work for a portion of expenses incurred in the care of their dependents, including children under age 15.

According to Sharon Stephan of the Congressional Research Service, other federal support for child day care includes funding for such services as the Child Welfare Services Program under Title IV-B of the Social Security Act, the Community Services Block Grant Program under the Human Services Reauthorization Act of 1986, the Community Development Block Grant Program under the Housing and Community Development Act, and the Dependent Care Planning and Development Program under the Human Services Reauthorization Act of 1986.

Additional federal assistance includes funding for employer-provided child or dependent care services under the Internal Revenue Code, and for such programs as the Indian Child Welfare Program, the Work Incentive Program, Aid to Families with Dependent Children, the Job Training Partnership Act, and the Food Stamp Program.

States' Role

But experts note that even though it is now the largest provider of such services, the federal government may not meet the growing demand for early childhood programs. It is in this climate that state governments, many of which traditionally have not funded prekindergarten programs, are assuming more responsibility for preschool education. Today, schools in more than two-thirds of the states offer some type of preschool program, according to High/Scope, and state funding independent of federal funding is a growing trend.

School officials seeking state funding for early childhood programs may investigate state education or social service agencies. States fund child care through the Federal Social Services Block Grant, though federal cuts in this program have forced many states to limit the number of children served, and through the federal Aid to Families with Dependent Children program. States may also provide child care assistance through tax credits, incentives to employers to subsidize child care or expand services, targeted child care aid for parents in training or education programs, and low-interest loans and rent assistance to child care providers. When funds are channeled directly to school districts, the programs usually follow the same school code provisions as those established for kindergarten, according to Carolyn Morado, early childhood supervisor for the **Ann Arbor, Michigan, public schools.** These programs may be offered by districts without seeking approval from the state department of education.

FEDERAL PROPOSALS

In 1987, 1988, and 1989, U.S. senators and congressmen debated several pieces of child care legislation. Before then, the last time a child care bill was passed by Congress was in 1971; but President Nixon vetoed it when it reached his desk. Among the major bills considered by the 100th and 101st Congresses:

- The **Act for Better Child Care Services.** The ABC bill was developed by a coalition of more than 70 child-welfare, education, women's, religious, and medical groups under the direction of the Children's Defense Fund. The 1989 bill sought $2.5 billion to create and subsidize child care programs for low- and middle-income families and the establishment of national health and safety standards for child care facilities.

- **Smart Start:** The Community Collaborative for Early Childhood Development and Child Care Assistance Act of 1988. (Senator Edward Kennedy, Democrat, Massachusetts). The Smart Start bill, which was introduced in the 100th Congress but failed to win passage, aimed to make high quality developmentally appropriate early childhood programs universally available. The bill called for federal funding to cover 70 percent of implementation costs the first year, 60 percent the second year, and 50 percent the third and following years, with states making up most of the balance. The U.S. Education Department would have made grants to states and localities through schools, Head Start Centers, and community organizations to provide full-workday, full calendar year programs to 4-year-olds.

Among other child care legislation proposed in the 100th and 101st Congresses were bills on parental leave, tax credits, and employer-assisted child care. Although none of the bills passed in 1988, observers believe the time is nearing for passage of a child care or early childhood education bill.

Special legislation

Schools can also investigate state funding tied to special legislation. Programs established through this channel are usually part-day and aimed at special populations, such as disadvantaged or English-as-a-second-language children. Special state-funded programs commonly require programs to meet specific standards related to staffing requirements: class size, staff-child ratios, age of children served, and eligibility criteria. Programs sites are usually determined through the awarding of grants to selected districts, often on a competitive basis. Many such programs in the pilot stages—namely those in California, New Jersey, New York, and Pennsylvania—have been operating for more than 10 years.

It is difficult to estimate typical state funding for prekindergarten programs, because figures are often grouped with those for kindergarten. In addition, direct state funding of early childhood programs is almost always supplemented by local support (cash or in-kind contributions) by school districts and other sources. Funding for programs created by special legislation, however, can be determined more easily since legislation generally defines the amount to be spent. Morado puts state funding at just under $1,000 per child for part-day programs, but notes that this funding may reach as much as $2,000 per child.

Local Funding

Local funding is playing a greater role today in light of federal budget cuts, and the emphasis during the Reagan Administration on initiatives emanating from the private sector and state and local governments. Those involved in child care and early childhood programs, having seen substantial federal infusions of money in the 1960s, are two decades later witnessing a return to local control, according to Jorde of the National College of Education. The early childhood community, she notes, is "reluctantly being forced to become more self-sufficient in meeting local needs by returning to its traditional grassroots model for program development and funding."[6]

Funding by Parents

Parental fees also support some early childhood programs — sometimes serving as the sole support of a program, but more frequently supplementing funding from other sources and often based on a sliding-fee scale dependent on family income. In January 1985, the costs to parents for day care in various major cities ranged from $35 to $175 per week for children from infants

Notes

1. Paula Jorde, "Early Childhood Education: Issues and Trends," *The Educational Forum*, Winter 1986, p. 172.
2. For more information on school-based child care programs for students, see "In School Together: School-Based Child Care Serving Student Mothers" (New York: Academy for Educational Development).
3. Seventeen states currently require local districts to provide noncompulsory kindergarten and assist with funding, according to the National Governors' Association. Districts in 27 states are permitted to provide kindergarten according to state law. And in three states, successful completion of kindergarten or passage of a readiness test is required for first grade admittance. Eight states require kindergarten attendance, up from one in 1982.
4. For more information on half- versus full-day kindergarten, see Sandra Longfellow Robinson, "Kindergarten in America: Five Major Trends," *Phi Delta Kappan*, March 1987; Dianne Rothenberg, "Full-Day or Half-Day Kindergarten," ERIC Digest (Urbana, Ill.: ERIC Clearinghouse on Elementary and Early Childhood Education, 1984); and Mary Renck Jalongo, "What Is Happening to Kindergarten?" *Childhood Education*, January/February 1986.
5. Gail E. Hanninen, "The Preschool Gifted and Talented Child," ERIC Digest (Reston, Va.: Clearinghouse on Handicapped and Gifted Children, 1985), p. 1.
6. Jorde, "Early Childhood Education: Issues and Trends," p. 173.

The Nuts and Bolts of Preschool Programs

"Quality early childhood education takes many forms, and quality programs may have different philosophies, goals, structures, and settings. There is no set formula."
—Daniel S. Cheever, Jr., president of Wheelock College in Boston, and Anne E. Ryder, a Wheelock graduate student and early childhood teacher[1]

Because early childhood programs vary considerably in both structure and content, those developing programs have a wide array of options to consider. A program may provide custodial care or stress academic preparation, run for part of the day or all of it, and group children by age or place them together without age consideration. Educators and others offering early childhood programs must consider such components as language development, grading and assessment, nutrition, parental involvement, and material selection.

To develop a better understanding of the parts that make up the whole that is an early childhood program—whether it be child care, kindergarten, or a Head Start class—consider the segments outlined in this chapter. They represent just some of the issues those establishing and operating programs must address at the start of the program and on a continuing basis in order to assure high quality.

PROGRAM STRUCTURE

Among the elements that make up a program's structure are those concerning format, length of day, age grouping, class size, and facility design.

Format

The format of an early childhood program—that is, what goes on during the program day—is most basic to the program and is usually determined by the sponsors' concept of its goals. Most programs include play and learning, and some feature more formal instruction.

Play

Play has been called the principal source of development in the early years. Since children learn through physical experience—tasting, touching, seeing, hearing, participating in activities—the opportunity to play is seen by child development experts as one of the key determinants of child care quality. "The play of children is not seen as a break from important work, but as the essence of the work itself," notes Ellen Galinsky, president of the National Association for the Education of Young Children and director of Work and Family Life Studies at Bank Street College of Education.[2]

High quality early childhood programs give children the opportunity to engage in constructive play, offering them many opportunities to select activities from a sufficient, though not overwhelming, number of choices, according to Galinsky. In addition, activities should be both child- and adult-initiated, take place inside and out-of-doors, and include both noisy and quiet varieties. And caregivers should be flexible enough to change activities according to children's needs.

Play also provides children opportunities to develop fine and gross motor skills through specialized and vigorous activities, work creatively alone and in group settings, observe processes, and engage in acting out daily experiences with which they are familiar. Children should also be given the freedom not to take part in a particular activity.

"A high quality child care environment is full of opportunity for new experiences," Asa G. Hilliard, III, Fuller E. Callaway Professor of Urban Education at Georgia State University, pointed out in his keynote address at the NAEYC's 1983 annual conference. "Piaget was right. The mental structures for thinking and action are not passed on from teacher to child in a package. They must be discovered anew by each child. Discovery is serious business."

The Westside Early Childhood Centers in **Omaha, Nebraska,** operate on a philosophy of "learning through play." The emphasis is on children making their own decisions as much as possible. "We want the child to learn how to learn, rather than learning to wait for an adult to direct him to a learning experience," Carolyn Law, principal and director of the program writes in a letter to parents.

As well, playing develops children's natural curiosity, allows them to explore concrete materials, and helps them develop self-confidence in their abilities. It also promotes problem solving, critical thinking, concept formation, and creativity. Social, emotional, as well as physical development are enhanced through play.

Intellectual approach

But spontaneous play is not the only component of a good early childhood program. Many believe that preschool programs should also feature an intellectually oriented approach in which children interact in small group settings to explore new and common experiences, observe, ask questions, experiment, and discover.

This intellectually oriented approach, however, does not include formal instruction. Although experts are divided as to whether preschoolers should receive formal schooling, most concur that formal group instruction with heavy emphases on reading, mathematics, and skills that are traditionally school-related is inappropriate and may create frustration in young children. "Academic pressures should never conflict with the young child's developmental needs," advise LaVisa Cam Wilson, professor in the Department of Curriculum and Teaching at Auburn University, and Neith Headley, an early childhood consultant and former kindergarten teacher.[3]

Others, however, believe there are benefits to early academic instruction. Although a minority, they are finding increasing support from parents who seek a head start for their children in today's competitive environment. Douglas Carnine of the University of Oregon contends that with 82 percent of fourth graders in the bottom quartile failing to complete school, there is no excuse for delaying academic instruction for those 5-year-olds who need it. (For a more detailed discussion of this issue, see Chapter 4.)

Curriculum

Regardless of their orientation, programs should be guided by a curriculum. For preschool programs, this means program administrators should devise a set of principles and goals that allow them to move through various stages of the program.

Officials who operate the **Flint, Michigan, community**

schools' prekindergarten program define curriculum goals as:
- Providing experiences that meet the physical, social, emotional, and intellectual needs of children.
- Providing activities that are appropriate for the children's individual levels of development.
- Developing positive feelings toward learning.
- Developing children's self-esteem.

To meet these goals, Flint educators plan specific learning experiences to promote children's skills in these areas:
- **Language**. The Peabody Language Kit, books, puppets, records, charts, field trips, and finger plays are used. An environment rich in language usage is provided.
- **Cognitive**. Experiences are offered that promote creative problem solving; decision making; and an understanding of shapes, colors, letters, and number and science concepts.
- **Large and fine motor**. Activities develop coordination of hand muscles through use of clay, peg boards, puzzles, crayons, scissors, pencils, paints, and other manipulative materials. Large motor skills are improved during outdoor play and through the use of climbing equipment, games, and music activities.
- **Socioemotional**. Activities in play and interaction with others encourage children to learn self-discipline, to express their ideas and feelings, and to function within a group.
- **Creativity**. Activities encourage a child's self-expression in the areas of art, music, story telling, and creative movement.

Successful curriculum models

When considering specific curriculum models for early childhood programs, schools are faced with a wide array of options. Just two examples are:
- The **Head Start** curriculum allows care givers to tailor activities to children's needs as well as to the ethnic and cultural characteristics of the community. Learning experiences are designed to foster intellectual, social, and emotional growth.
- The **High/Scope Educational Research Foundation's** curriculum introduces children to words and numbers, colors, shapes, animals, safety precautions, and other types of knowledge and awareness by allowing them to plan and carry out activities on their own. Guided by Piaget's theories, the curriculum attempts to find the best ways to support and extend children's emerging skills.

Curriculum organization

With any curriculum, administrators and teachers should consider three components—learning centers, skills groups, and units of study, according to Barbara Day, professor and chair of Teaching and Learning, School of Education, University of North Carolina at Chapel Hill. Each of these parts should be organized to teach specific topics such as self-concept, language arts, or animal habitats, Day notes.

Day also recommends attention to classroom management, including the use of color coding to organize instructional materials and games, pictorial or written contracts to help direct children's learning, and a clear understanding and execution of discipline methods.

A number of early childhood program administrators find it helpful to set forth curriculum objectives. **Lamar Consolidated School District** officials in **Rosenberg, Texas,** for example, have designated school, self-awareness, and family as the curriculum units that are covered during the first six weeks of their prekindergarten program. These are communicated to parents so they can help further their children's learning. Also communicated to parents are the specific skills students will be exposed to, including:
- Saying their first and last names.
- Saying the teacher's name.
- Touching and counting three blocks.
- Naming eight body parts.
- Sequencing three pictures.

Curriculum units for Lamar's kindergarten program cover mathematics, language arts, science, social studies, and health. In the curriculum area of science, for example, students are given the opportunity to:
- Identify eyes, ears, skin, nose, and tongue as body parts used for senses.
- Apply knowledge of light to seeing.
- Identify sources of sounds.
- Recognize that vibrations cause sounds.
- Identify objects by feel and by their odors.
- Identify food according to taste.
- Identify body parts and parts of the face.
- Describe what can be done by body parts.

Reading

Just as the early years are important to children's social, emotional, and physical development, so are they important in their development of literacy. Despite general agreement on this point, however, there remains considerable controversy surrounding the issue of when and how to teach children to read.

In *Stages of Reading Development*, Jeanne S. Chall, professor of education and director of the reading laboratory at the Harvard

University Graduate School of Education, outlines a six-stage developmental scheme—from pre-reading to highly skilled reading. The pre-reading stage, which early childhood educators see most often, starts at birth, continues to age six, and is characterized by children's increasing control over language, according to Chall. During this stage, most children discover printed words; learn to recognize letters, common signs, and common words; and may be able to write their own names.

Educators and caregivers often ask whether they should teach children to read or allow them to read and figure out the process on their own. Research, says Chall, supports the use of both methods for optimal reading development. Chall also supports the evidence that the use of challenging materials that are somewhat above children's reading levels produce higher reading achievement than easy books, especially when there is accompanying teacher instruction.

In an effort to address appropriate reading readiness in pre-first grade programs, the Association for Supervision and Curriculum Development, the International Reading Association, the National Association for the Education of Young Children, the National Association of Elementary School Principals, and the National Council of Teachers of English issued a joint statement of concerns about present practices and recommendations for future improvement. Among the recommendations in "Literacy Development and Pre-First Grade," prepared by the Early Childhood and Literacy Development Committee of the IRA:

- Reading and writing experiences at school should permit children to build upon already existing knowledge of oral and written language.
- Learning should take place in a supportive environment so children can build a positive attitude toward reading.
- For optimal learning, teachers should involve children actively in many meaningful, functional language experiences—including speaking, listening, writing, and reading.
- Teachers of young children should be prepared in ways that acknowledge differences in language and cultural backgrounds and emphasize reading as an integral part of the language arts as well as of the total curriculum.
- Teachers should encourage risk-taking in first attempts at reading and writing and accept what appear to be errors as part of children's natural patterns of growth and development.
- Children should be encouraged to read for pleasure so they associate reading with enjoyment.

Writing as a way to help children learn to read has gained popularity among educators in recent years. Based on the premise that children build knowledge from their own activities, those who

FAIRY TALES

Hansel and Gretel, Rapunzel, Snow White, Little Red Riding Hood, Cinderella. Beyond their role as enticing stories, fairy tales encourage children to fantasize, to use their imaginations, and to learn to find and use their creativity. This is the theory of Bruno Bettelheim, renowned educator and psychologist. In *The Uses of Enchantment: The Meaning and Importance of Fairy Tales*, Bettelheim chronicles fairy tales' role in enriching children's lives.

The most important and difficult task in child raising, says Bettelheim, is helping children find meaning in their lives. One of the most effective ways to help them find that meaning, he notes, is through good literature that arouses curiosity, stimulates imagination, clarifies emotions, and recognizes difficulties, while also suggesting solutions to problems.

Consider "Hansel and Gretel," which chronicles a child's striving to hold on to his parents when the time has come for setting out in the world alone. This tale, Bettelheim suggests, offers a lot to the young child ready to make his first steps into the world, the child of about four or five. Among its messages is reassurance that fears of desertion, over-dependency, and starvation, even in their most exaggerated form, prove unwarranted. The children are victorious in the end and the most frightening enemy, the witch, is defeated.

"Today children no longer grow up within the security of an extended family, or of a well-integrated community," he notes. "It is important to provide the modern child with images of heroes who have to go out into the world all by themselves and who, although originally ignorant of the ultimate things, find secure places in the world by following their right way with deep inner confidence."

SOURCE: Revised and reprinted with permission from *The Uses of Enchantment: The Meaning and Importance of Fairy Tales*, by Bruno Bettelheim, 1976. Copyright (c) 1986 by Alfred A. Knopf, Inc., New York, N.Y.

support writing to teach reading believe children should be given opportunities to write whatever and however they choose using different types of paper and writing utensils.

Computers

For the teacher or administrator who has just gotten used to having, or paying for, a computer in the 10th-grade math classroom, the idea of computers in the child care center might seem surprising. But computers are becoming more readily accepted as important and useful additions to preschool and kindergarten classrooms.

Teachers who use computers say they provide opportunities for individualized instruction at each child's pace, foster active learning, excite children, and—when used well—promote autonomy, self-esteem, and cooperation. Working with different types of software, children can play games that help them learn numbers, words, shapes, and other concepts; color with a joystick; play tunes to develop hearing skills; solve problems; and get quick feedback and replay.

In the **Orangeburg, South Carolina, School District 5,** Superintendent James Wilsford has used technology, especially computers, extensively in the highly successful "Project Education Reform." For example, kindergartners who score "not ready" on the Cognitive Skills Assessment Battery (CSAB) use IBM software called Writing to Read. The software is based on getting children to read words they already know verbally. According to Wilsford, "Teaching kids to read becomes much easier. They're writing their own stories and reading their own stories."

Computer use among preschoolers is not without criticism, though. Among the questions raised: Can young children who have not yet reached the stage at which they can perform concrete operations work meaningfully with computers? Does computers' reinforcement of rote memorization harm learning? Will computers usurp teachers' roles and consume time as adults learn to operate, teach, and program for individual needs? Does developmentally appropriate software exist?

Those considering computer use in the preschool classroom should begin by determining what role they wish the computers to play. In many schools, purchase often comes before planning. Educators should then choose what kinds of software will meet their purposes, noting that "the effectiveness of any software will be influenced by the age and experience of the child using it," according to Mima Spencer, an expert on computers in schooling.[4]

Among basic options: highly structured software, which provides a limited number and variety of responses, has acceptable answers to pre-programmed choices, and requires children to match responses in computer memory rather than create their own (computer games and drill and practice programs, for example); and less-structured software that encourages self-expression or invites creative responses (simulations and LOGO, for example).

High quality software programs share certain characteristics, says Spencer. Consider whether the software contributes to children's comprehension of the world around them. Does it both foster and satisfy curiosity? Does it require a high degree of interaction from the children, call for thoughtful responses, and provide options that require choices? Are clear directions for running the program provided, and does the program consistently respond as expected? "A well-designed, easy-to-use program with interesting content that also shows awareness of children's love for the ridiculous, the repetitious, or the surprising is a find," according to Spencer. "When choosing software, look for programs that reflect understanding of children, and invite children to contribute from their own experience."[5]

Educators looking at software might also consider the results of the "Survey of Early Childhood Software," an annual study conducted by the High/Scope Educational Research Foundation. In 1988, the survey tested 286 programs for their ease of use, level of interactivity, technical features, content strength and presentation, feedback techniques, and level of child-control. Based on these criteria, along with thorough classroom testing, the survey selected six software packages as the best. Those identified are:
- Color Me, by Mindscape.
- Explore-a-Story Series, by D.C. Heath & Company.
- Mask Parade, by Springboard Software.
- Math and Me, by Davidson Associates.
- Muppets on Stage, by Sunburst Communications, Inc.
- Observation and Classification, by Hartley Courseware, Inc.

Before purchasing any software, experts recommend previewing it. In this way, it is possible to determine whether the program works with the school computer and whether it is appropriate for students' age levels before paying for it.

Length of Day

If the curriculum guides a preschool program, it is the length of the program day that shapes it. As discussed in Chapter 2, most child care programs operate on a full-workday basis, while those that are of an early intervention or educational nature usually operate for part of the day, requiring parents to find alternative care to supplement the program.

The length of day issue involves a host of other questions,

including that of developmental appropriateness. Many question whether very young children should attend highly structured academic full-day programs. Others are concerned about children's ability to spend so much time away from home and fear that full-day programs may be too stressful and exhausting for children. These concerns contribute in large part to the current debate between proponents of half-day kindergarten and those of full-day kindergarten.

In deciding how long programs will run, administrators would be wise to determine whether their programs represent a solution to existing child care problems or contribute to the problem. Those with half- or full-school-day programs might consider implementing supplemental care to meet parents' needs for full-workday care, or assisting parents in finding and transporting children to community providers that offer such care.

Class Size

The length of the program day is not the only structural component of early childhood programs that has been the focus of public attention. Since the start of the recent education reform movement, class size has topped the list of recommendations at all levels.

State and local policy makers have in the past few years legislated, suggested, and regulated that class size—especially in the early years that are so important to later development—be reduced and that student-teacher ratios be limited. Smaller classes, the argument goes, mean more individualized attention for children. That, in turn, means more opportunity for learning and development.

The link to achievement

A study released in 1986 provided support for those seeking to lower class size in kindergarten programs. The study, published by the Chicago Board of Education, is thought to have been the first to measure kindergarten achievement in full- and half-day and large and small classes. Its findings: Class size is more important than the length of school day in the achievement of disadvantaged kindergarten children. It is the quality of time spent with children, not the quantity, that is most important. Simply lengthening school days can be disadvantageous unless there is adequate funding to hire additional caregivers to reduce class size.

Other child care studies have also supported the benefits of small groups. The 1979 National Day Care Study found that the quality of care is highly related to the number of children in groups. In small groups, caregivers spent more time interacting

- If absent eight consecutive days and the teacher has not been notified of the reason for the absence.
- For irregular attendance, such as attending one or two days a week for a month.
- If the child is left at school after dismissal time.
- If there is no record of a physical or health screening within four weeks of enrollment.
- If there is no record of immunizations within four weeks of enrollment.
- If the parent and teacher have not been able to solve extreme behavior problems.
- If the family moves from the attendance area of the school.

Information sheets should also include guidelines for payment practices—that is, whether checks are accepted, to whom they should be made payable, whether scholarship aid is available, and what penalties are incurred for late payment. Programs open to low-income children may require that parents interested in enrolling their children submit financial information—paycheck stubs, W-2 forms, or Welfare Department forms.

Parents brochure

Many early childhood programs also find it useful to distribute to parents information covering a wide range of additional practical matters, including:
- Program goals and objectives.
- Discipline procedures.
- Parent conference sessions.
- Parent-involvement options.
- Suggestions for home learning activities.
- Testing and assessment practices.
- Hours, transportation alternatives, and vacation schedules.
- Information on health matters.
- Policies on clothing. Is there a dress code? What should children wear when playing outside, when working on art projects, when going on field trips?
- What children can bring from home. Many programs allow children to bring one or two small objects from home (toys, pictures, etc.), provided they are labeled and kept in children's storage areas when not in use.
- Any additional items children can or should bring from home, such as mats, bedrolls, pillows, art supplies, and so forth.
- Meal times and sample menus.
- Nap times.
- A typical schedule for a program day.
    Clues for designing a typical schedule for any early childhood

program might be garnered from the Nebraska Department of Education's guidelines for kindergarten planning for half-day programs, as outlined in "Planning the Use of Time in the Kindergarten":
- **Arrival**.
- **Planning time** (15 minutes). When children participate in opening routines (roll, flag, milk count, etc.), present experiences or items they have brought to share, hear about new or special activities in work areas, and individually plan activities and materials to be used that day.
- **Work time** (50 minutes). When children carry out plans for the day in the various work areas (sociodramatic, blocks, art, manipulatives, language, math, music, science, etc.), work alone or with a friend, and work with the teacher individually or in small groups (dictating, practicing a new skill, etc.).
- **Snack time** (15 minutes). When children experience new food tastes, textures, etc.; learn about nutrition; socialize with friends; learn self-help skills; practice good manners; and practice math skills by helping prepare and distribute snacks.
- **Active play time** (20 minutes). When children move freely using their whole bodies in indoor and outdoor settings, play age-appropriate group games, use playground equipment, and play cooperatively.
- **Quiet time** (15 minutes). When children listen to the teacher read; look at books; listen to records, tapes, etc.; and use quiet materials individually.
- **Group time** (20 minutes). When children participate in group singing, fingerplays, saying poetry, playing rhythm instruments; hear from special visitors—community workers, adults with special talents; learn about group participation; go to the school library; dictate group experience charts; look at audiovisual presentations (educational television, films, etc.); participate in group dramatic activities; and learn about new concepts.
- **Time for evaluation** (15 minutes). When children verbalize in the group setting what they have done or learned, share things they have made, plan for future activities, begin to appreciate another's point of view, and remember what they need to take home (notes, pictures, experience stories, etc.).
- **Departure.**

PROGRAM COMPONENTS

Among the elements considered program components—or what goes into an early childhood program—are those concerning health and safety, nutrition, language development, parental involvement, multicultural issues, assessment, discipline, and materials. (The role of the teacher is, of course, central to the effectiveness of early childhood programs; for a thorough discussion of this issue, see Chapter 5.)

Health and Safety

Health and safety considerations in preschool programs take several forms. In addition to safety concerns, there are emergency procedures; policies needed for illness in children, spread of disease, admission of children with AIDS and AIDS-related complex, and child abuse; medical check-up requirements; and related program content. (Although there are no national child care health standards at this time, a set of standards for health, safety, sanitation, and nutrition was drafted in 1989 by the federal Bureau of Maternal and Child Health.)

Safety

The most basic safety considerations relate to the daily environment of program participants. Facilities should be designed and planned based on a good understanding of children's needs and abilities. In addition to sufficient space, there should be adequate heat, light, and ventilation.

Preschool facilities should have smoke detectors, fire extinguishers, and safety caps for electrical outlets. Each room occupied by children should have posted instructions on how to respond to emergencies and should have a first-aid kit, according to the American Academy of Pediatrics. Staff members should be trained in first aid and cardiopulmonary resuscitation, and should have parents' telephone numbers as well as information on hand for reaching emergency contacts.

Among other considerations that may be somewhat different from regular K-12 situations:

- Those working with children should wash toys and hands frequently.
- Bathrooms must be especially clean and accessible to children.
- Food, including snacks, requires proper storage.
- Seat-belt regulations should be instituted and enforced on field trips. Additional state and local transportation regulations should be met to ensure safety.
- Playground and other equipment must be selected appropriate to the age group enrolled and properly maintained. (Since the U.S. Consumer Product Safety Commission has found that more than 70 percent of play equipment injuries result from falling, children should be supervised at all times.[7])

- School personnel should know what adult is picking up each child at the end of the program day, and should be alerted when someone other than the usual person will be performing that duty. To facilitate this, programs can adopt a sign-in and sign-out procedure: Each child is signed in upon arriving at the center and signed out upon leaving; adults accompanying children perform the signing and must be authorized to do so on enrollment forms. Special precautions should be taken to ensure that only a parent with legal custody is allowed to pick up a child, unless the legal parent has signed a statement agreeing to other arrangements.
- Parents should be notified as to appropriate dress. Young children who are prone to accidents should have an extra set of clothing at the center. Children taking part in cooking or other potentially dangerous activities should be dressed appropriately.

Medical considerations

Recent media attention has focused on the health risks of child care, namely that children participating in child care programs suffer from more infections and colds than those who do not. Because there is some truth to the fact that colds and viruses spread quickly among children, programs that enroll young children should require that both children and adults have regular check-ups. They should also formulate a policy regarding treatment of children who become ill during program hours. Some centers, for example, require that parents pick up children who become ill within two hours of diagnosis by school medical staff.

Center policies of this type should be included in information on health regulations and practices sent to parents at the start of the program year. It is also helpful to require parents to sign forms attesting to their understanding of these regulations and procedures. In **Fairfax County, Virginia,** for example, the Office for Children, which operates preschool and extended-day child care programs called SACC (School-Age Child Care Center) requires parents to complete a "Permission for Emergency Care" form. Included on the form are the parents' names, addresses, and telephone numbers; the names, addresses, and phone numbers of other emergency contacts; and the child's physician's name and telephone number. The form also includes information about any allergies, handicapping conditions, or contagious diseases the child may have. And it asks for the names of any medications the child is taking. Parents are asked to sign the form, attesting to their understanding of such center policies as:
- No medication will be administered without written permission from parents and written instructions from a physician.
- Children cannot attend SACC if they have any illness that

threatens the health of other children.
- Health Department regulations concerning periods of infecton will be enforced.

The form includes the following statement, to be signed by the parent:

> The SACC Center [School-Age Child Care Center] has my permission, in an emergency when I (or my physician) cannot be contacted, to take my child to the emergency room of the nearest hospital, and the hospital and its medical staff have my authorization to provide treatment which a physician deems necessary for the well-being of my child. The original of this [form] shall be readily accessible in the SACC Center, and taken to the hospital with the patient. (The copy shall be placed in the Office for Children files.)

Parents who enroll their children in an early childhood program also are usually asked to complete a "permanent health record," which requests a child's history of immunizations, including date of each dose; and the parents' assessment of the child's health, behavior, and ability to get along with others.

This form often includes a section, to be completed by the child's health care provider, on medical tests and screenings, medication, disabilities, allergies, and special health considerations.

In addition to the emergency and health record forms that are submitted upon enrollment, many programs require parents to submit a written request for program staff to administer any type of medication. In Ohio, for example, the state requires the use of a form called, "Request for the Administration of Medication by Child Day Care Personnel." Parents of children in day care centers and certain family day care homes who are taking medication, vitamins, or food supplements, or who are on modified diets, must have their physicians complete the form, which includes:

- Physician's instructions for medication.
- Specific instructions for administration.
- Possible side effects to watch for.
- Expiration date.
- Physician's signature.

If the medication or vitamins have been prescribed by a pharmacist, the parent can complete the form. The form also contains a list, to be completed by day care personnel, of the date, time, and dosage of medicine administered.

At the Kiddieland Express Day Care Center, a program for 2-and-a-half- to 5-year-old children that is operated by the **Delight, Arkansas, public schools,** parents are advised as follows:

Medication will be given only if parents complete the medication form provided at the center. Please notify us if your child has a contagious disease so that we may alert other parents. Sick children should not be brought to the center until the contagious period is over and the child can resume normal activities. If a child becomes ill during the day, the parents will be notified. Parents are encouraged to include in the child's records a set of instructions to be followed in an emergency situation. This information should state the doctor and the hospital preferred and [give] authorization for treatment in your absence.

In devising local health policies, program administrators advise checking appropriate state and local laws, keeping accurate medical records, and urging parents to update files regularly.

Going beyond forms

Some programs, especially those for low-income children who do not have regular access to health services, take an extra step in health care. They contract with community doctors to provide screening and treatment for health problems as well as immunizations at regular intervals throughout the program year.

The **Flint, Michigan,** Head Start program, for example, provides dental examinations with cleaning, topical fluoride applications, and bitewing x-rays through a community health center and private dentists. In addition, all children enrolled in the program are required to have physical examinations or health screenings by the health department or their private doctor. Parents are assisted, if necessary, in securing follow-up treatment for identified treatable problems, and made aware of available community health resources.

Flint Head Start also provides immunizations and screenings, as needed, for:

- Tuberculosis tests
- Sickle cell anemia
- Hemoglobin/hematocrit
- Vision and hearing
- Speech

- Diphtheria/tetanus
- Oral polio
- Measles
- Rubella
- Mumps.

(Sample health and accident forms are located in Appendix III.)

Policies on AIDS

With the advent of AIDS as an important health issue, schools are also beginning to develop written policies regarding admission of children with AIDS or AIDS-related complex (ARC). Although it is difficult to devise blanket regulations to cover all possible cases of children with AIDS, adoption of a policy statement covering general guidelines should be done before officials have to deal with their first case.

Many public schools today have developed or are developing such policies, but changes may have to be made for programs admitting very young children for a number of reasons: Young children are more likely to have AIDS or ARC as a result of having been born with the disease, and they are more prone to accidents that involve the risk of loss of bodily fluid.

When formulating policies for preschool programs, it should be kept in mind that none of the reported cases of AIDS in the United States have been transmitted in schools or day care centers, according to the National PTA. Furthermore, the Surgeon General, the Centers for Disease Control, the American Academy of Pediatricians, and the PTA believe that most children with AIDS or ARC should be in school, based on physicians' approval.[8]

School officials formulating a policy statement on AIDS might consider including some of the following items, suggested by administrators who have adopted such policies:

- Cases will be considered by a team consisting of the child's parents, his or her physician, a public health official, and a school official.
- Each case will be considered separately according to the individual child (his or her age, control of bodily functions, etc.) and setting.
- Children with open sores, young children who lack control of bodily functions, those prone to biting, and certain others may be considered for alternate school sites (school-based tutors, home tutors, etc.).
- Mandatory screening of all children for AIDS will not be undertaken.
- Recommendations for treatment of adult cases of AIDS or ARC should also be addressed in policy.

The American Association of School Administrators has published a book, *Dealing With AIDS, Breaking the Chain of Infection*, which outlines an AIDS education program that can be taught within the framework of a comprehensive K-12 health education program. For early elementary school children, AASA recommends that AIDS education should be designed to allay excessive fears of the epidemic and of becoming infected. For very young children, the message is simple and nonspecific.

Child abuse policies

Those administering preschool programs should also be guided by policies related to child abuse. Although the American Human Society reported in 1985 that only 1.5 percent of all reported cases of child abuse take place in child care settings, this reality, plus

> # SAMPLE POLICY FOR STUDENTS WITH INFECTIOUS CONDITIONS OR AQUIRED IMMUNE DEFICIENCY SYNDROME (AIDS)
>
> *Policy*: To the maximum extent possible under guidelines published by the Centers for Disease Control and the American Academy of Pediatrics, students will be included in all school programs for which they are eligible. Only after the following steps are taken shall a student be excluded from the classroom for continuing infectious conditions such as Hepatitis B or HIV infections.
> 1. The superintendent will ask the interdisciplinary team to convene for the purpose of making a recommendation concerning the educational environment. The student may be excluded from school pending the completion of this process.
> 2. The interdisciplinary team will include the following personnel: a physician with expertise in immunology and/or communicable disease; the public health medical director; supervisors of the school health program from the health department and the school district; a representative of upper level administration from the school district; and the General Director of Education for Exceptional Students. The superintendent will determine if legal council or other persons will be present.
> 3. The team will meet with the parents, the student's

public concern, warrants precautions.

Consider, for example, the findings of researchers from the University of New Hampshire and its Family Research Lab. In the first national study of sexual abuse in child care, they reported that there were four allegations of abuse for every one substantiated case.

The researchers also reported that only eight percent of abusers in their study had records of official sex offenses. For this reason, they suggested, preschool administrators should not rely on criminal record checks alone for screening potential abusers. Nor should they rely on licensing agents because agents lack the time and sometimes the training to detect abuse. Instead, program administrators should check references thoroughly before hiring.

Among other recommended precautions:

> attending physician, the principal of the student's school and others the parents may wish to include (i.e. student, legal council).
> 4. The team will follow a written protocol which will be made available to all participants and will use the most recent Centers of Disease Control and Academy of Pediatrics guidelines in considering the case.
> 5. The team will make its recommendations to the superintendent within two weeks or give written reasons why this is not possible.
> 6. The superintendent will forward the team's recommendations to the school board.
> 7. Every reasonable effort wil be made to respect the student and family rights to confidentiality and privacy.
> 8. If the decision is made to exclude the student from the classroom, services appropriate for the student will be provided in a homebound or other more restrictive setting.
> 9. All cases will be reviewed by the team every six months or more frequently if requested by the parents, school personnel, or team members.
> 10. The superintendent will direct appropriate school personnel to assist parents who request that their HIV infected students be exempted from compulsory school attendance. (Legal Reference: FS 232.06)
>
> SOURCE: Hillsborough County Public Schools, Tampa, Fla.

- Hire an adequate number of staff members, since abuse is less likely to occur when there are several staff members taking care of children.
- Do not release children to adults other than custodial parents, unless those parents provide written consent.
- Adopt written procedures for dealing with suspected cases of abuse.
- Ensure that staff members understand their legal obligations to report abuse.
- Provide staff training to help teachers recognize signs of abuse.
- Never restrict parents from stopping by unannounced.[9]

Also of interest: In 1987, the National Association of State Boards of Education and the American Association of School Ad-

SAMPLE LETTER TO PARENTS ON SUSPECTED CHILD ABUSE

In a booklet entitled, "Parent's Guide to Day Care," the licensing branch of the Texas Department of Human Resources, like other state human resource and social service departments, outlines guidelines for parents adaptable to most early childhood programs:

Most day care facilities, like most parents, take good care of children. Child abuse is rare, and it is very unlikely that anything like this will happen to your child.

If you do suspect that your child has been physically abused or sexually molested, report the situation immediately. Use the toll-free Child Abuse Hotline number, available 24 hours a day. If you think the abuse occurred in a day care facility, call your day care licensing office. The situation will be investigated immediately, and you will be given referrals or recommendations for help for your child and family.

Again, sexual and physical abuse are rare. However, if your child volunteers information about abuse, you need to take this seriously. Parents who suspect or believe that their child has been abused in day care sometimes remove their child from care, but don't report the problem. This leaves other children in danger. State law requires you to report suspected child abuse. Should testimony in court be needed, you may be able to testify on behalf of your child if you were the first person to hear your child's story. When a person makes a report of suspected child abuse or neglect in good faith, he is immune from any civil or criminal liability. If a complaint is made with malicious intent or for revenge, there is no liability protection.

When the department investigates a complaint, the identity of the complainant is not revealed. *Everyone, including day care providers, is required by law to report suspected child abuse or neglect immediately.* The best of parents sometimes become angry, frustrated, and upset with their children. Sometimes, circumstances, like financial or marital problems, seem overwhelming, and parents fear that they may lose control and hurt a child. Help is available in your community. Don't wait until a tragedy occurs. Call for assistance.

ministrators released a joint statement on the prevention of child sexual abuse in public schools. Aimed at producing more formal, strengthened, and widely communicated policies on child abuse, the statement includes guidelines for local school districts on staff hiring procedures, reporting and handling allegations of abuse, and dealing with the outcomes of investigations. In another action, the National Association of State Directors of Child Development adopted a resolution in 1986 calling for more federal research on the incidence of intra- and extrafamilia child sexual abuse; more federal assistance in training local personnel involved in the detection, apprehension, disposition, incarceration, and treatment/ rehabilitation of child sexual abusers; and more federal assistance to improve data collection at the national, state, and local levels to facilitate the retrieval of data related to abuse.

Insuring Early Childhood Programs

The insurance crisis

In 1985, child care centers began to report problems in obtaining insurance coverage. Program operators found their center policies cancelled mid-term and then renewed. Replacement policies were difficult to find and extremely costly, with increases soaring to 600 percent. Those insurance companies that continued to offer coverage generally attached stringent eligibility criteria.

The crisis affected all sorts of programs, regardless of claims history, years of operation, or program quality. Public schools also felt the squeeze, whether they offered early childhood programs or not. Mainly affected were high-risk activities and programs.

At first glance, the insurance crisis seemed linked to concern over sexual abuse cases in day care, but the American Human Association noted that only 1.5 percent of cases occur there. And the National Association for the Education of Young Children and numerous state surveys pointed to the lack of data to support the insurance industry's claim that child care was a high risk. The insurance industry in turn was unable to produce evidence of large claims at the request of children's advocacy groups, Congress, and the U.S. General Accounting Office.

It seemed, instead, that interest rate declines that caused the insurance industry to suffer major losses in investment income were behind the unprecedented increase in rates and the cancellation of policies that were perhaps less risky than unprofitable.

The effect was devastating, forcing many programs to close and others to go dangerously without insurance. Still others had to cut corners on program quality in order to afford insurance payments.

Today, despite tort reform, self-insurance, and other reform proposals, and despite an easing of the crisis, insurance problems—especially reduced coverage and increased limitations on the amount of coverage—continue to plague the early childhood field, according to Jim Strickland, executive director of Child Inc., and a leading analyst of the insurance situation. In addition, many of the insurance companies that returned to child care after the initial crisis found they could make large profits and subsequenty lowered their prices. That, says Strickland, could contribute to a return of market instability.

Nonetheless, insuring early childhood programs is essential. It is also required by certain states as a condition of licensing. Although most early childhood programs are safe—especially those established in public schools that are already aware of safety regulations and needs—young children are more prone to certain accidents than older children. And accidents do happen, as anyone who works with children knows.

What insurance should cover

In a study of more than 400 injuries to preschoolers in Los Angeles child care centers in 1983 and 1984, researchers from the School of Public Health at the University of California, Los Angeles, cited electrical outlets and playground equipment as danger areas. Therefore, preschool programs should ensure that liablity insurance for property and center covers areas inside and outside the building. Insurance should also cover field trips away from the program site; school transportation used by students; and visits by preschoolers to other parts of the school building, if the program is located in an existing K-12 or K-6 site. Consider, too, purchasing for automobile, workers' compensation, and student accident medical coverage, as well as coverage for child abuse or sexual molestation.

For more information on insuring preschool programs, consult:
- The schools' existing policy and insurer.
- The State Office of Insurance or State Insurance Commissioner.
- The NAEYC (see Appendix I for address).
- The Child Care Action Campaign (see Appendix I).

Nutrition

Unlike most elementary and secondary school programs, early childhood programs usually provide meals and snacks. The American Academy of Pediatrics recommends that children in programs for nine or more hours a day be given at least two meals and two snacks. Timing of the meals and snacks is dependent on program day, arrival and departure schedules, and related factors.

Because there is a proven link between nutrition and mental ability, programs for at-risk children should ensure that some portion of children's daily nutritional needs are met. Head Start participants receive a minimum of one hot meal and one snack per day, meeting at least one-third of their daily nutritional requirements.

The pediatricians also recommend:
- Planning meals and snacks with the assistance of a dietician (particularly helpful for school officials interested in adapting existing K-12 food programs to young children).
- Featuring selections from the four major food groups.
- Never using food as reward or punishment.

In addition, parents should be provided information about the food that is served. This way, they can alert program administrators of any food allergies or diet restrictions their children might have.

One other important consideration to keep in mind when planning snacks or meals relates to our increasingly pluralistic society. Because more and more children are representing a wide variety of religious and ethnic groups, program administrators should be aware of dietary restrictions and preferences and deal with them appropriately.

Programs should also feature discussions about nutrition, teach children the basic elements of healthy eating, and help underscore the importance of proper dental care. Head Start children, for example, learn about healthy eating and have regular dental checkups. Parents are taught by trained nutritionists how to plan and prepare healthy, low-cost meals at home.[10]

The Flint, Michigan, prekindergarten program publishes these guidelines for mid-morning and mid-afternoon snacks. Two of four of the following components must be served at that time:
- A serving of fluid milk (1/2 cup).
- Enriched or whole-grain bread (1/2 a 25-gram slice), cereal (1/3 cup or 1/2 ounce), cooked pasta or noodle products (1/4 cup), cooked cereal grains (1/4 cup).
- Cooked meat or meat alternate (poultry, fish, cheese) (1/2 ounce), eggs (1/2 egg), cooked dry beans or peas (1/8 cup), peanut butter (1 tbsp.)
- Full-strength juice (1/2 cup) or fruit or vegetable. (Juice and milk cannot be served together to meet snack requirement.)

Language Development

Language is the instrument through which teaching takes place, whether it be formal or informal instruction. And promoting the development of language in children should be one of the primary goals of early childhood education, according to Barbara Simmons, associate dean and professor of education at Texas Tech University, and JoAnne Brewer, assistant superintendent for instruction in **California's Hesperia Elementary District.**

In a 1985 article in *Childhood Education*, Simmons and Brewer point to research showing that classrooms that do not stimulate talking retard language development, and that teachers who encourage verbal interaction help children improve their communications skills.

Another study of children in child care, this one by Kathleen McCartney, assistant professor of psychology at Harvard University, found that a high degree of verbal interaction between children and their caregivers not only promotes youngsters' acquisition of language, but influences their positive emotional development.

Among the activities that encourage language development in preschoolers:
- Reading books.
- Telling stories, including those that involve personal experiences.
- Engaging in informal conversation.
- Listening to adults and other children.
- Answering open-ended questions.
- Labeling items.
- Identifying objects and words.
- Singing.
- Playing with puppets and other materials.

Language acquisition objectives

The **Rialto, California, Unified School District** publishes lists of "Expectancies for Student Achievement" for kindergartners. Speaking and listening expectancies indicate students at all grade levels will:
- Listen with purpose and speak with influence.
- Listen to and participate in classroom activities/discussion.
- Expand knowledge and use of language with a variety of strategies and media.

At the kindergarten level, students will:
- Listen to and follow directions.
- Listen and respond to literature, media, and other verbal presentations.
- Recite prose and poetry.
- Articulate feelings and needs.
- Describe, classify, or compare objects, people, places, and experiences.

Note how these kindergarten objectives differ somewhat from those prepared by the Oklahoma Department of Education for programs for 4-year-olds. Guidelines for listening suggest that by the end of the school year, children will:
- Talk and listen when in a large group.

- Follow two directions in sequence.
- Recognize and name common environmental sounds.
- Differentiate between different sounds.
- Imitate and repeat simple rhythm.
- Recognize some sounds that rhyme.

Guidelines for speaking note that children will:
- Refer to self in the first person.
- Express ideas in complete sentences of six or more words.
- Use past and future tenses and form plurals correctly.
- Name objects rather than just pointing to them, saying, "I want that."
- Ask simple questions using who, where, what, and why.
- Give relevant answers when asked questions.
- Carry on conversations with adults and peers.
- Begin to put ideas and events in correct sequence when relating personal experiences.
- Retell familiar stories in correct order.
- Interpret pictures verbally.
- Participate in simple finger plays and songs.

(For more information on the expected skills and behavior of young children, see Chapter 4.)

Parental Involvement

Most educators recognize the importance of parental involvement in K-12 education. The involvement of parents plays an even greater role in preschool programs.

Parental involvement, according to researchers and educators, reinforces parents' role as their children's first teachers; helps them play a greater role in their children's subsequent schooling; and gives children a secure sense of home-school continuity. According to David Weikart and Lawrence Schweinhart of High/Scope: "At best, caregivers join with parents in a mutual give-and-take concerning the child's development and learning."

(For a more thorough discussion of parental involvement, turn to Chapter 6.)

Multicultural Issues

Depending on a child's home life, an early childhood program may represent the first exposure to multicultural issues. It is at this time that many children first become aware of racial, ethnic, and religious differences. The early childhood setting can provide a good starting point for multicultural education, says Hakim M. Rashid, professor of early childhood education at Jackson State University.

"As children move from the home to the early childhood education setting, their views of ethnic, racial, and religious groups will either be reinforced or challenged by the 'curriculum' to which they (and their families) are exposed," notes Rashid. "Thus the totality of experiences in early childhood education...all contribute to the shaping of the young child's conception of the culturally different."[11]

Early childhood educators have an opportunity to introduce their students to a rich variety of historical and cultural perspectives and events. The American Association of Colleges of Teacher Education has developed guidelines for teacher education programs seeking to include a multicultural perspective. They include:

- Preservice teacher education curricula should prepare students to teach from a multicultural perspective and to work effectively with all students regardless of their ethnic backgrounds, sex, age, socioeconomic level, or personal handicaps or strengths.
- The general studies component should provide the opportunity for students to study cultural diversity from both historical and contemporary perspectives, including how that diversity has contributed to the development of and been affected by our society.
- The professional studies component should include experiences that allow students to understand cultural diversity and its implications for the development of appropriate teaching strategies.
- The teacher education faculty should reflect the institution's commitment to multicultural education.
- Faculty with expertise in aspects of multicultural education should serve as a resource for schools in the area served by the institution.
- The institution should provide the faculty with opportunities for developing and implementing innovations in multicultural education.
- The teacher education program should be designed to help teachers work well with a culturally diverse student body.
- The program should also contain an ongoing, systematic assessment plan for evaluating and improving its multicultural education thrust.

Among the many ways preschool programs can facilitate multicultural awareness are:

- Celebrating holidays of various cultures.
- Reading letters and diaries of leaders and ordinary people of years and cultures of the past.
- Cooking and serving foods from various regions.
- Inviting parents and others to share cultural experiences (arts, crafts, music, dress, and stories of their cultures).
- Visiting museums and other community cultural resource centers.

Bilingual education

In addition, based on the idea that language plays an important cognitive role in children's development, some contend that bilingual education is an important element in early schooling. Research, they note, supports the soundness of adopting a bilingual approach along with a bicultural approach, for those for whom English is not the native language—as well as for those whose native language is English.

Grading and Assessment

Educators accustomed to traditional methods of assessing children at the elementary and secondary levels will have to reconsider the issue as it relates to younger children. In most cases, developmentalists agree, standardized paper-and-pencil tests are inappropriate for evaluating the development of preschoolers and kindergartners, as well.

In 1988, the NAEYC and the National Association of Early Childhood Specialists in State Departments of Education teamed up to urge schools to stop using standardized tests to determine promotion and retention of kindergartners. "Our children are being tested too early and failed too soon, and parents should ask for what purpose," said Sue Bredekamp, NAEYC's accreditation director. "The most important things to learn in kindergarten cannot be measured on a standardized test, so there is little or no educational reason for the testing, yet it is happening all over the country." Early standardized testing takes place in preschools, too.

The stress factor

This kind of testing is sharply criticized by many developmentalists who charge traditional tests are too stressful. Instead of traditional tests, experts urge evaluators to use observation by teachers or other trained observers based on a set of standards for quality. Among the existing measures of quality are the Early Childhood Environment Rating Scale (Harms & Clifford, 1980), the NAEYC Standards of Program Quality (1984), and the High/Scope Preschool Implementation Profile (for programs using the High/Scope curriculum). These and other measures address the elements of program structure outlined above, plus such components as materials, parental involvement, teacher training, and evaluation. (See Chapter 4 for more discussion on student testing.)

Developmental criteria

If tests are used, they should be appropriate for the kind of program offered and the children's levels and diversities. They should meet criteria for developmental and predictive validity and for reliability, and they should never serve as the sole basis for decisions related to admission or placement.

Progress reports and specially prepared report cards can be instrumental in charting children's development in early childhood programs. The **Alief, Texas, Independent School District** sends report cards every six weeks to the parents of 4-year-olds enrolled in its prekindergarten program. The reports reflect overall progress in specific curricular areas. Children's progress is also monitored through daily work and parents are encouraged to meet with staff members at least twice yearly.

Program administrators can encourage parents to play a role in the assessment of their children's development by scheduling teacher-parent conferences at regular intervals, as the Alief schools do. They can also encourage parents to ask questions about the program, observe work their children have done, and discuss events in children's lives. Working with parents to assess children's social, emotional, physical, intellectual, and cognitive development can help administrators and teachers develop curricula, identify children with special needs, and evaluate programs. (See Chapter 8 for further discussion on testing as a part of program evaluation.)

Discipline

Discipline as an issue in early childhood programming is quite different than it is for high school and even elementary school classrooms. Since preschoolers are at a developmentally different stage than older children, appropriate discipline is important.

In developing an approach to discipline for young children, program administrators should take into consideration each child's developmental age, the kinds of discipline they receive at home, and the goals of the program. They would also be wise to take into account the advice of Alice S. Honig, an expert in children's programs.

According to Honig, author of an NAEYC pamphlet entitled, "Love & Learn: Discipline for Young Children," children imitate our behavior and live up to our expectations. Teachers should therefore set reasonable and positive expectations, respect children's feelings, and provide a safe environment conducive to growth and development. Furthermore, Honig notes, children should be given choices, told which behaviors are acceptable and which are not, and trusted to succeed.

In **St. Louis, Missouri,** the Afton-Lindbergh Early Childhood Education Program at Harry S Truman Middle School outlines the following discipline policy:

At Afton-Lindbergh Early Childhood Education, teachers courage children to respect the rights, property, ideas, and feelings of others. Students learn to exchange points of view and to resolve problems and conflicts independently. Expectations and guidelines are clearly explained, so students learn that they can depend on the consistent support of adults.

Materials and Equipment

Early childhood programs require a wealth of materials and equipment in order to provide an environment suitable to curious children with large appetites for exploring the world around them. All materials, the experts suggest, should be developmentally appropriate. This means that photocopies of worksheets are poor substitutes for cups, sand, and water when introducing children to the concept of measurement. Developmentally appropriate materials often cost more than those that are inappropriate, but they represent wise investments in children's development.

Materials should be easily accessible and grouped according to function. Among the materials in a good preschool program: artistic tools, musical instruments, tapes and records, construction materials, sand, water, clay, dress-up costumes, outdoor climbing and play equipment, rocking toys, dolls, stuffed animals, and books.[12] As well, athletic equipment such as a balance beam can be fun and provide exercise for children.

Kathleen Haug, in her guidebook on designing children's learning environments, suggests materials that can contribute to a block and construction experience center. This type of center, she recommends, should be away from the main traffic area so that projects are not disturbed and should be carpeted for noise absorption. Pictures can be mounted on the walls to provide children with ideas or themes for construction. The equipment needed includes:
- Unit blocks.
- Hollow wood blocks.
- Large cardboard blocks.
- Form blocks.
- Giant Legos.

Accessories to add to this collection include:
- Cars, trains, trucks, planes, and boats.
- Wood or vinyl animals.
- Ramps, boards, and planks.
- Wood traffic signs.
- Wood or vinyl people and community helpers.
- A steering wheel, pulley, and tire pump.

- Pieces of hose and rope.
- A flashlight, binoculars, spy glass, and periscope.
- A blanket to be used as a roof.
- A wooden box with dials and switches.
- Life preservers.
- A small canoe paddle and fishing poles.
- Various types of hats.

In a similar way, Haug suggests the development of a music experience center, to include such equipment as a bongo, snare, or tub drum, maracas, tambourines, rhythm sticks, sand blocks, cymbals, triangles, hand bells, and other instruments. Accessories for a music center might include wands, colored scarves, records, and tapes.

Preschool programs make great use of basic materials such as paper and glue. For this reason, some programs ask parents to purchase materials at various intervals throughout the year. The **Alief, Texas, Independent School District,** for example, provides parents with a "Prekindergarten Supply List." Each child should bring to the program:

- Two large primary pencils with erasers.
- A pack of eight large crayons.
- An 8-ounce bottle of white liquid glue.
- A pair of plastic safety scissors, left-handed if necessary.
- A 5-ounce jar of paste.
- A folder with pockets.
- A regular-sized box of tissues.

Among the books available in a preschool program should be those that are well-known to most children (to reinforce the home/school tie); those that are new and provide opportunities for exploration; picture books and books with differing amounts of text; and books of poetry and nonfiction, as well as fiction and fairy tales.

Program administrators and teachers seeking appropriate materials for preschool programs should be prepared to enter a market that is quite different than that of elementary and secondary textbooks and other resources. Publishers have not yet moved to provide a large variety of preschool books, and traditional children's literature books can be expensive. Teachers and administrators of early childhood programs should work to ensure that adequate books are produced and made available for affordable prices; and they should try to convince parents and school board members of the merits of using alternative materials that are of high quality.

EQUIPMENT CATALOGS

The following is a list of some catalogs containing information on equipment suitable for early childhood classrooms. **It is not intended as an inclusive list of equipment suppliers.** (Listings marked with an asterisk [*] carry teaching aids, also.)

Community Playthings*
Route 213
Rifton, New York 12471

Constructive Playthings
1227 E. 119th St.
Grandview, Missouri 64030

The Growing Years
Childcraft Education Corp.
20 Kilmer Road
Edison, New Jersey 08818

ABC School Supply Inc.
6500 Peachtree Industrial Blvd.
P.O. Box 4750
Norcross, Georgia 30091

Play Learn Catalog
Division of PCA Industries, Inc.
2298 Gussom Drive
St. Louis, Missouri 63146

Nienhuis Montessori USA, Inc.
320 Pioneer Way, Dept. 4
Mountain View, California 94041

Minnesota Valley School & Office Supply
P.O. Box 255
St. Peter, Minnesota 56082

Jonti-Craft Inc.
P.O. Box 30, Hwy. 68
Wabasso, Minnesota 56293

Hobbitat*
Westbrook Mall
5717 Xerxes Ave. North
Minneapolis, Minnesota 55430

The Learning Center, Inc.*
224 Bates
St. Paul, Minnesota 55106

New Generation Toys
290 Larkin St.
Buffalo, New York 14210

Kaplan School Supply Corp.
600 Jonestown Road
P.O. Box 15027
Winston-Salem, North Carolina 27102

Child's Play Central
P.O. Box 448
Eureka Springs, Arizona 72632

Lakeshore Curriculum Materials Co.
P.O. Box 6251
Carson, California 90749

SOURCE: *A Guide for Designing the Children's Learning Environment of an Early Childhood Family Education Program and Additional Resources,* by Kathleen Haug, Copyright © 1985 by the Minnesota Department of Education.

Notes

1. Daniel S. Cheever, Jr., and Anne E. Ryder, "Quality: The Key to Successful Programs," *Principal*, May 1986, p. 19.
2. Ellen Galinsky, "Promoting Positive Growth in Children Is No Accident," *Index: Child Care*, June 1987, p. 4.
3. LaVisa Cam Wilson and Neith Headley, "Working With Young Children" (Wheaton, Md.: Association for Childhood Education International, 1983), p. 4.
4. Mima Spencer, "Choosing Software for Children," ERIC Digest (Urbana, Ill.: ERIC Clearinghouse on Elementary and Early Childhood Education, 1986), p. 1.
5. Spencer, "Choosing Software for Children," p. 2.
6. Joan Moyer, Harriet Egertson, and Joan Isenberg, "The Child-Centered Kindergarten," position paper of the Association for Childhood Education International, *Childhood Education*, April 1987, p. 239.
7. For guidelines on construction, location, and installation of playground equipment and surfacing, contact the U.S. Consumer Product Safety Commission. For help in spotting unsafe conditions and a free, confidential consultation in which citations are not issued, contact the Occupational Safety and Health Administration of the U.S. Department of Labor.
8. For more information, send for a free copy of the 36-page "Surgeon General's Report on Acquired Immune Deficiency Syndrome" (write to AIDS, P.O. Box 14252, Washington, DC 20044) or the Red Cross's "AIDS and Children: Information for Teachers and School Officials" (contact local Red Cross offices or the American Red Cross, AIDS Education Office, 1730 D St., N.W., Washington, DC 20006; single copies are free).
9. For more information on the study, see Karen Stephens, "The First National Study of Sexual Abuse in Child Care: Findings and Recommendations," *Child Care Information Exchange*, March 1988.
10. For more information on food in early childhood programs, consult the food program requirements of the U.S. Department of Agriculture's Child Care Food Program. Write Samuel P. Bauer, Director, Child Nutrition Division, USDA, Food and Nutrition Service, Room 509, 3101 Park Center Drive, Alexandria, VA 22302.
11. Hakim M. Rashid, "Multicultural Issues in Early Childhood Education," in Kevin J. Swick and Kathryn Castle, eds., *Acting on What We Know: Guidelines for Developing Effective Programs for Young Children* (Little Rock, Ark.: Southern Association on Children Under Six, 1985), p. 62.
12. For more information on toy ideas for children from birth to age six, see "Toys: Tools for Learning," a brochure published in 1985 by the NAEYC. See also Kathleen Haug's *A Guide for Designing the Children's Learning Environment of an Early Childhood Family Education Program and Additional Resources*, published in August 1985 by the Minnesota Curriculum Services Center, which is supported by the State of Minnesota Department of Education and the State Board of Vocational Technical Education.

Developmental Appropriateness: What It Is, Why It's Important

"Every time you *tell* a child something, you rob him of the opportunity to *discover* it for himself."
—Bertha Campbell, former director of New York State's experimental preschool program

We know that early childhood programs—whether for toddlers, 4-year-olds, or kindergartners—are best when they operate based on the ways young children develop and learn. We also know that preschool-age children learn differently than do older children, acquiring the skills necessary to learn by interacting with the environment around them instead of assimilating specific pieces of knowledge through formal thought processes. But even among their own age group, factors exist that cause them to learn, behave, and grow at different rates from each other. Parents and educators of preschool-age children must pay attention, then, to the different stages children go through in developing early childhood programs.

The Pitfalls of Inappropriateness

Research has shown that when children, especially the very young, are forced to learn concepts before they are ready, they may suffer from stress, inattention, or a lack of self-esteem. They may even experience physical problems such as nervous disorders, poor eyesight, and inadequate neurophysical coordination. In *Miseducation: Preschoolers at Risk*, David Elkind, professor of child study and resident scholar at the Tufts University's Lincoln Filene Center for Citizenship and Public Affairs, points to long-term motivational, intellectual, and social problems as additional risks of inappropriate early education.

Similarly, in a 1983 cover story called, "Bringing Up Superbaby," *Newsweek* magazine noted that inappropriate early learning can be highly stressful and may create problems later in life. Acknowledging that scientists don't know exactly how knowledge gets into the brain, the article noted that information learned under unpleasant or stressful conditions never reaches the memory banks. Early learning through inappropriate methods, then, may turn children away from the joys of learning and squelch their natural curiosity, souring them on learning experiences throughout life.

In one expert's opinion, programs based on curricula or teaching methods that focus inappropriately on narrowly defined intellectual achievement risk wasting the promise of early childhood education. High quality prekindergarten programs should not be watered-down versions of third grade, and good preschool teachers should recognize the importance of focusing on children's own interests to a greater degree than third grade teachers. "Unless schools and teachers observe these distinctions," he holds, "we risk losing the developmental potential of early childhood education in a misplaced effort to mass-produce little Einsteins."

Pressure for Academics

Despite these cautions, support for what some consider inappropriate programs that focus on academics and formal instruction comes from many sectors. Among them: parents eager to provide their children with the early start that has been linked to later school success, and who equate learning and development with academics. Says Robert Cervantes, director of early childhood education for the California Department of Education: "Parents want their kids to read, write, and speak two languages when they hit kindergarten."

Support also comes from a public that believes children of the 80s and 90s, with access to television, computers, and other media, are somehow more intellectually advanced than their parents and grandparents were at the same age. It comes from those convinced that we must take advantage of the fact that children's intellectual capacities develop considerably from birth to age five and from educators used to academic programs. And it comes from legislators eager to turn public interest, and money, into visible programs that produce equally visible results.

"Many programs...are thriving from coast to coast as if educators had never heard of child development," noted Constance Kamii,

> ## THE BUTTERFLY
>
> I remember one morning when I discovered a cocoon in the back of a tree just as a butterfly was making a hole in its case and preparing to come out. I waited awhile, but it was too long appearing and I was impatient. I bent over it and breathed on it to warm it. I warmed it as quickly as I could and the miracle began to happen before my eyes, faster than life. The case opened; the butterfly started slowly crawling out, and I shall never forget my horror when I saw how its wings were folded back and crumpled; the wretched butterfly tried with its whole trembling body to unfold them. Bending over it, I tried to help it with my breath, in vain.
>
> It needed to be hatched out patiently and the unfolding of the wings should be a gradual process in the sun. Now it was too late. My breath had forced the butterfly to appear all crumpled, before its time. It struggled desperatley and, a few seconds later, died in the palm of my hand.
>
> That little body is, I do believe, the greatest weight I have on my conscience. For I realize today that it is a mortal sin to violate the laws of nature. We should not hurry, we should not be impatient, but we should confidently obey the eternal rhythm.
>
> SOURCE: *Zorba the Greek*, by Kazantzakis.

professor at the University of Alabama's education school, in a 1985 keynote address at the annual conference of the Chicago Association for the Education of Young Children. These programs, which "force-feed" isolated skills to children and focus on worksheets and pencil-and-paper exercises, are wholly inappropriate, Kamii noted. But they are popular, she said, because they provide educators with the impression of teaching toward a clear objective in well-planned sequences. They keep children quiet and save teachers time. They are also more easily "graded" and offer parents and the public quick feedback on children's progress.

Programs that place preschoolers in traditional classrooms, then, seated at desks with worksheets, memorization lessons, and teacher-directed instruction, are not conducive to learning for most young children. Their focus on the three R's—areas in which preschoolers have little interest—is often to the exclusion of opportunities for the natural discovery and exploration processes so important to children's development.

WHAT IS "DEVELOPMENTALLY APPROPRIATE"?

Just what is developmentally appropriate? In 1986, the NAEYC conducted an extensive review of relevant research and solicited input from hundreds of early childhood professionals to find the answer to this question. The results of their efforts were published in a position statement that includes guidelines for developmentally appropriate practice in curriculum, adult-child interaction, home-program relations, and evaluation of children.

Developmentally appropriate programs should:
- Emphasize the process of learning rather than the result.
- Accept the stage children currently occupy rather than the level at which adults may want them to be.
- Help children acquire confidence in their ability to develop skills and learn about their environment.
- Feature developmentally appropriate materials—which are often more costly than traditionally academic materials—to encourage children to discover and explore.
- Allow children to direct their own learning, with guidance from teachers.

The High/Scope Educational Research Foundation, author of the Perry Preschool Study, agrees with those who caution against formal schooling in preschool. In a 15-year study of preschool curricula, the group found that children who take part in preschool programs that allow them to initiate their own activities are more likely to be involved in school activities and to be seen positively by their families. They are also less likely to become involved in anti-social activities, crime, and delinquency.

"These long-term results should give pause to public school educators who want to extend academic schooling down to age four," said David P. Weikart, president of High/Scope, on releasing the report, "Consequences of Three Preschool Curriculum Models Through Age 15," in 1986. "While good early childhood programs can help improve the life chances of disadvantaged children, formal academic programs with highly directive teachers may not produce the desired effect on social behavior."

Schools ignore the basics of developmental appropriateness when they "push pencil and paper tasks on young children; [don't] understand a developmental, intellectual [versus traditionally aca-

CONTRASTS BETWEEN DEVELOPMENTAL SCREENING TESTS AND READINESS TESTS

	Developmental Screening Tests	Readiness Tests
Purpose	To identify children who may need early intervention or special education services. To identify children who might profit from a modified or individualized classroom program.	To facilitate curriculum planning. To identify a child's relative preparedness to benefit from a specific academic program.
Content	Items that display a child's ability or potential to acquire skills.	Items that focus on current skills achievement, performance, and general knowledge.
Type of Test	Norm-referenced.	Most are criterion-referenced; some are norm-referenced.
Psychometric Properties	Reliability. Predictive validity.	Reliability. Construct validity.

SOURCE: Samuel J. Meisels, "Uses and Abuses of Developmental Screening and School Readiness Testing," *Young Children*, January 1987, p. 5.

Readiness tests

The **Ulysses School District No. 214** in **Ulysses, Kansas,** defines school readiness as "the ability to cope with the school environment physically, socially, and emotionally, as well as academically, without undue stress, and to sustain in that environment." This district operates a program for youngsters who are of the right age to enter kindergarten, but whose parents wish to delay their entry for a year. The program focuses on language acquisition and socialization skills, with activities designed to promote each child's success in school.

Readiness tests, testing expert Samuel J. Meisels notes in the an article in the January 1987 issue of *Young Children*, have to do with those curriculum-related skills a child has already acquired, skills that are typically prerequisite for specific instructional programs. Used to judge a child's readiness to enter a particular program or grade, the test informs placement decisions as well as curricula. Children who are said to be unready for entrance are recommended for deferral, retention, placement in an alternative program, or enrollment in a transitional class between traditional grades or programs.

An example of a readiness test is the Gesell School Readiness Test, which addresses various facets of children's development. The test is used by the **Lincoln Parish School District** in **Ruston, Louisiana,** to screen all entering kindergarteners during the first two weeks of the school year. Administered one-on-one by a trained examiner, the test seeks to determine whether the child's overall development, or developmental age, is consistent with, below, or above his or her birth age. On the basis of the test, one of three determinations is made: that the child stay home, that he or she participate in developmental kindergarten, or that he or she take part in regular kindergarten. Parents who disagree with the evaluation may discuss it with school faculty; and an appeals process allows further discussion, according to Supervisor Brenda Theodos.

Other examples of readiness tests for preschoolers and early elementary students include:
- The First Grade Screening Test, published by the American Guidance Service.
- The Metropolitan Readiness Test and the Boehm Test of Basic Concepts, both produced by Psychological Corporation.
- The Cognitive Skills Assessment Battery, published by Teachers College Press.
- Circus, administered by the Educational Testing Service.

Concerns About Testing

Despite their popularity, readiness tests have come under attack by a number of educators concerned with their effect on children's lives. In 1987, the National Association of Early Childhood Specialists in State Departments of Education, in a strong condemnation of schools' use of such procedures, called heightened readiness standards inappropriate and the practices they have inspired possibly counterproductive.

Others assail readiness tests because:
- They focus on children's current achievement levels to the exclusion of their developmental potential.
- Such early testing fails to recognize that young children are not good test-takers.
- The risks of misdiagnosing are considerable. In some instances, children who are not learning disabled but are merely "developmentally young" are the victims of inappropriate labeling and

subsequent placement that affects them for years.

The American Academy of Pediatrics cautions: "Results of intelligence, maturation, and development tests should be interpreted cautiously. Almost all are culture-biased and subject to misinterpretation." The group adds: "There are no absolute indicators for kindergarten or nursery school readiness."

On the other hand, screening procedures may lead to misevaluation and poor placement of children. Therefore, perhaps the most important considerations in determining whether and how to use both screening and readiness tests are reliability and validity. "During the years," Meisels notes in the *Young Children* article, "professionals have misused and abused both screening and readiness tests. Because young children grow and change so rapidly from day to day and week to week, it is critical that tests used to assess these children be stable and accurate."[5]

Some Evaluation Methods that Work

In his book, *Developmental Screening in Early Childhood: A Guide*, Meisels suggests that high quality tests:
- Meet the acceptable criteria of standardization, reliability, and validity set by the American Psychological Association in 1985.
- Focus on developmental rather than academic tasks.
- Be brief.
- Represent a multidimensional sampling of a wide range of developmental areas.
- Include an appeals process that allows parents to question results.

Meisels identifies four screening instruments he believes meet these requirements. The tests, individually administered developmental screening tests, are:
- The Denver Developmental Screening Test, which Meisels calls the best-known and most widely used developmental screening instrument. Its wide age range (two weeks to six years) allows screening over a period of years.
- The Early Screening Inventory, which he calls an easily learned, brief screening instrument that samples developmental, rather than school achievement, abilities and focuses on performance in a wide range of developmental areas.
- The McCarthy Screening Test, which Meisels calls a "promising instrument" that may be more discriminating for academically and developmentally advanced children than other screening tests.
- The Minneapolis Preschool Screening Instrument, which Meisels says includes a higher proportion of classroom readiness tasks than most developmental screening tests and is a good predictor of learning problems for at least a one-year period.[6]

WHAT SCHOOL LEADERS CAN DO

Efforts to ensure that preschool programs are developmentally appropriate must involve educating the public about the differences between early childhood education and formal schooling. They should also include providing information about the appropriate content of programs for young children.

"The school board, superintendent, and principal should stand firm in insisting on a program that helps children do *children* things—not pressure them to do *school* things," says Sava.[7] Adds Elkind: "Sound early childhood education is an extension of the home, not of the school."[8]

Notes

1. Lilian G. Katz, "What Should Children Be Learning?" *ERIC Digest* (Urbana, Ill.: ERIC Clearinghouse on Elementary and Early Childhood Education, 1987), pp. 1-2.
2. Sue Bredekamp, ed., *Developmentally Appropriate Practice* (Washington, D.C.: National Association for the Education of Young Children, 1986), p. 3.
3. Mary Hatwood Futrell, "Public Schools and Four-Year-Olds: A Teacher's View" (Washington, D.C.: National Education Association, undated), p. 3.
4. A list of curriculum materials and their prices can be obtained by writing to Early Prevention of School Failure, 114 N. Second St., Peotone, IL 60468, or by calling (312) 258-3478.
5. Samuel J. Meisels, "Uses and Abuses of Developmental Screening and School Readiness Testing," *Young Children*, January 1987.
6. Meisels, *Developmental Screening in Early Childhood: A Guide* (Washington, D.C.: National Association for the Education of Young Children, 1985), pp. 32-39.
7. Samuel G. Sava, "The Endangered Promise," in Lawrence J. Schweinhart, *A School Administrator's Guide to Early Childhood Programs* (Ypsilanti, Mich.: High/Scope Educational Research Foundation, 1988), p. viii.
8. David Elkind, "Formal Education and Early Childhood Education: An Essential Difference," *Phi Delta Kappan*, May 1986, p. 636.

Children's Caregivers: Early Childhood Staff

"There can be no more important subject from the standpoint of the nation than that with which you are to deal, because when you take care of the children you are taking care of the nation of tomorrow."
—President Theodore Roosevelt, opening address to delegates to the First White House Conference on the Care of Dependent Children, January 25, 1909

The relationship between staff members and young children in early childhood programs is said to be the single most important determinant of program quality. Given its importance, the field has seen efforts in recent years to beef up standards for teacher preparation and training, certify more child care workers, and pay caregivers and preschool teachers higher salaries.

WHO STAFFS PRESCHOOL PROGRAMS? TEACHERS/CAREGIVERS

The Census Bureau and the National Association for the Education of Young Children counted 1,390,000 child care workers in 1984. Of those:
- 383,000 worked as caregivers in private households.
- 677,000 were employed in educational and social service settings.

- 330,000 worked as prekindergarten and kindergarten teachers.

These figures, however, probably underestimate the actual number of early childhood workers—given gaps in reporting (particularly among unlicensed day care homes) and definition. NAEYC estimates the number of those providing direct services to children is closer to 2.8 to 3.4 million.

Early childhood staff members fall under a number of categories. The NAEYC, whose membership consists largely of child care providers, defines a four-level early childhood professional path:

- **Early childhood teacher assistant.** Pre-professionals who implement program activities under direct supervision (an entry-level position for those with a high school diploma and no specialized early childhood preparation).
- **Early childhood associate teacher.** Professionals who independently implement program activities and who may be responsible for the care and education of a group of children (for individuals with a Child Development Associate credential or an A.A. degree in early childhood education/child development).
- **Early childhood teacher.** Professionals who are responsible for the care and education of a group of children (for those with a baccalaureate degree in early childhood education/child development).
- **Early childhood specialist.** Professionals who supervise and train staff, design curriculum, or administer programs (for those with a graduate degree in early childhood education/child development or early childhood teachers with three years of experience).

In other programs—Head Start, for example—staff members are identified as professionals (teachers), support staff who work on a paid basis as cooks, custodians, secretaries, etc., volunteers (parents or community members), and medical professionals.

Whatever the titles and positions, there is considerable variation in the educational backgrounds of early childhood staff, particularly those in non-school settings. This diversity is the result of such factors as differences in certification requirements, regulatory standards, and opportunities for inservice training from one area to another, as well as the salaries paid to staff members.

There is usually less variation in education among teachers who work in school-based early childhood programs, especially if those programs are run by the school board or established as a result of legislative action. Teachers in these programs can be required to meet local or state certification requirements. However, programs can be housed in school buildings but administered by community organizations or agencies that don't require certification.

tency-based assessment system that identifies, evaluates, improves, and recognizes individual competencies and abilities in early childhood workers. The Child Development Associate (CDA) program awards credentials to those individuals who meet program requirements. The program is administered by the Council for Early Childhood Professional Recognition, a subsidiary corporation of the NAEYC. As of January 1984, 27 states and the District of Columbia had incorporated the CDA into their state licensing regulations as an option for preschool qualifications.

Teacher Training for Early Childhood Versus Elementary Education

Barbara Bowman, director of graduate studies for the Chicago-based Erikson Institute, a Loyola University affiliate and a recognized authority on teacher training issues, points out some additional issues. Prospective prekindergarten teachers, she says, should participate in training that recognizes the differences between teaching elementary school students and teaching preschool children. To achieve this, Bowman advises that training programs should:

- Include a much greater emphasis on parent education, involvement, and communication than programs for elementary school teachers. Half of teachers' work in early childhood programs should be with the parent; this is even more important for children with special needs.
- Reflect the differences in how curriculum content is used in programs for young children. In the early years, teachers use content as a vehicle for building structures (for example, they teach the alphabet not so that children learn each letter, but so that they learn about the alphabet as a whole and what it represents). Later, teachers fill that structure with content (by teaching specific letters to make up the alphabet).
- Understand that motivation is far more important with young children than it is with older youngsters. "Teachers have to be much more in tune with what turns kids on," and understand how to make use of children's natural interest in play as a key to learning.
- Recognize that the organization of preschool programs differs from that of elementary programs. "It has to be much more flexible than [programs] for older children." Instead of learning just how to plan programs, then, teachers should be able to recognize various stages of children's development in order to be able to respond in timely fashion with the appropriate material.

Bowman says some colleges of education have incoporated into their teacher-training programs courses that recognize these differences, but state requirements make it difficult to cover all the

LILIAN KATZ ON TEACHER TRAINING

Public school prekindergarten teachers **should receive generic teacher-training** skills similar to those taught to prospective elementary teachers. But they should also learn other skills key to working with young children. That's the view of Lilian Katz, director of the ERIC Clearinghouse on Elementary and Early Childhood Education and an expert on early childhood programs.

Prospective prekindergarten teachers, Katz says, **should take part in practicums to obtain experience** working with prekindergarten-age children. They should also work on developing skills for interacting with parents; the younger the children, the more important that teachers have this skill, Katz says. "It matters so much," she notes, adding that it is difficult to learn this type of skill theoretically. Instead, she suggests a practicum addressing this area that is led by an experienced teacher.

Since prekindergarten teachers usually work in teams with at least one other adult (an aide or another teacher), students preparing to work in prekindergarten programs **should also learn how to work with other teachers**, focusing on learning how to cooperate and coordinate their work with others. And since prekindergarten teachers do not teach specific subject-area classes, as elementary teachers do, "you've got to be a really good generalist, to learn to work with an integrated curriculum," advises Katz.

Finally, prospective preschool instructors **must learn observation skills**, "how to get a good picture of a child's total functioning," says Katz. Teachers who lack observation skills may mislabel a child, locking him or her into a lasting pattern; or may miss important clues to a child's development that indicate it's time to intervene with special services.

bases. In addition, prospective teachers have more to learn today. "The job's harder, there's no doubt," Bowman says. In this climate, she advises considering teacher education as a starting point and ensuring that there are strong inservice components for teachers once they begin working.

Staff Development/Inservice Training

Efforts to upgrade training and certification in the early childhood field extend beyond teacher-training institutions into regular inservice training sessions, so staff members can keep abreast of new developments and maintain continued interest and enthusiasm. Given variations in the quality of preservice training, many in the field look to inservice training as an important component of a high quality program.

"Inservice training is a must for early childhood staff," according to Lawrence J. Schweinhart, director of the Voices for Children project of the High/Scope Educational Research Foundation.[7] Preschool program directors, he says, should schedule training sessions at least once each month.

A variety of approaches

In 1986, 26 states required some form of ongoing staff development. Requirements in the 26 states range from 3 hours annually to 15 hours worth of courses per year and 2 hours per month, according to Gwen Morgan, author of the NAEYC's "The National State of Child Care Regulation, 1986." While there are no field-wide standards governing staff development, the NAEYC's governing board is reviewing the issue.

For those working in public school prekindergarten programs, staff development most often takes the form of visiting other programs and attending conferences, according to the Bank Street College of Education/Wellesley College "Public School Early Childhood Study." For others, staff development takes a variety of forms:

- The **Lansing, Michigan, public schools'** preschool and kindergarten teachers take part in inservice meetings that focus on child growth and development, classroom management, stress management, discipline, and activity planning, according to Linda Kent, program development specialist.
- Teachers in **Columbus, Ohio**, who work with the district's latchkey program, receive inservice training on program development, how to interact successfully with children of different ages, and first aid; according to Patricia Townsel, kindergarten resource teacher.
- In the **Ferguson-Florissant, Missouri, School District**, local

programs based on the state's "Parents as Teachers" project are "especially good because of all the time we have devoted to staff support and development," according to Marion Wilson, early education director. There, the staff holds weekly meetings and participates in curriculum writing and summer workshops.
- Teachers in the **Fort Sam Houston, Texas, Independent School District's** preschool programs for 3- to 5-year-old handicapped children and 4-year-old bilingual, English-as-a-second-language, and disadvantaged children are trained by the U.S. Army. Based on standards developed by the Armed Forces, the program covers safety, first aid, and child development.
- **Michigan's Mason Community Education District** provides preschool and kindergarten teachers sessions on such topics as pre-writing, developmentally appropriate practice, and the importance of certain types of play. Day care providers also meet with staff from other area programs, according to Betsy Landy Cline, who says she hopes to encourage participation in meetings and resource sharing.
- Under the sponsorship of the California State Department of Education, a five-year pilot training program for infant and toddler caregivers is being carried out in four regional sites across the state. Developed by the Far West Laboratory for Educational Research and Development, the new program is designed to ensure high quality infant care for mothers who must work outside the home, and uses video and written material in English, Spanish, and Chinese.

Teachers also take part in inservice programs offered by state departments of education, local universities or training centers, and state or national organizations. For some, tuition reimbursement is provided or course credit is accepted by the district.

ONGOING CONCERNS

Staff development programs should give teachers an opportunity to discuss issues that come up in daily classroom work, provide emotional support, and promote professionalism. In doing so, they can focus on any of a number of areas, including:
- Assessment, observation, and evaluation of both children and the program).
- Teaching strategies.
- Learning styles.
- Language development and literacy.
- Recognizing and reporting child abuse and neglect.
- Curriculum development and goals.
- Materials selection and use.

- Community perceptions and support.
- Changes in program style or management.
- School-home relations and parent involvement.
- Problem areas.

Preschool administrators can add to the effectiveness of staff development sessions by presenting guest speakers and allowing opportunities to review recent child development research and discuss current issues in the field.

Improvements Hindered

Efforts to upgrade training programs for people who work with children have been hindered, in part, by the myth that early childhood workers need no formal training and, since the profession is female-dominated, that caring for children comes naturally. It has been noted that former president Reagan cyrstallized these attitudes in 1981 when he stated that, "Mothers and grandmothers have been taking care of children for thousands of years without special college education."

Also hindering training is a failure to recognize the differences between the skills needed to teach 3- and 4-year-olds and those needed for elementary school children. Although some states offer special credentials for caregivers based on the specific level they will teach, others fail to differentiate between age groups. In addition, there are teacher training programs that overlook differences and schools that assign elementary teachers to preschool programs, a practice that has been called "questionable" as well as "a cause for great concern."[8]

Addressing this concern, Mary Hatwood Futrell, past president of the National Education Association, advises: "Early childhood professionals and [public-school] teachers will have to unite and insist that [school-based early childhood] programs be staffed by professionals fully trained and prepared to cope with the special needs of preschool youngsters."[9]

State and local regulations

Those attempting to improve training have also come up against problems caused by great variations in state regulations that set guidelines for those who work with children. For example, only 28 states require prekindergarten teachers to have special training in early childhood education, according to a 50-state survey conducted in 1986 by Randy Hitz of the Oregon Department of Education.

There are also variations in local district requirements. Only half of all district-level respondents to the "Public School Early Childhood Study" indicated that early childhood education certification was a type of certification required for teachers in their programs.

As efforts to upgrade training and certification continue, many of today's caregivers are less qualified than those who entered the field 10 years ago. "We're getting less and less qualified people," says Neugebauer. Despite scattered tightening of requirements—which sometimes pushes people away from the field instead of drawing them closer—there has been a decline in the quality of staffers, much of which can be traced, according to Neugebauer, to the overall teacher shortage.

A FINAL NOTE

Fostering productive, sympathetic relationships between young children and their caregivers is one of the most important responsibilities of maintanining an early childhood education program. "It is through this relationship that children learn about themselves; whether the caregiver does this formally or it just happens, children derive feelings about themselves from their contact with the caregiver," according to Ellen Galinsky, NAEYC president and director of Work and Family Life Studies at Bank Street College of Education. "It is also through this relationship that children learn about their world—facts, figures, and concepts that enable them to understand more about how their world works. Finally, it is through this relationship that children learn about the processes of learning: how to tackle something new, how to organize their thinking, and how to solve problems."[10]

Notes

1. Barbara Willer, "The Growing Crisis in Child Care: Quality, Compensation, and Affordability in Early Childhood Programs" (Washington, D.C.: National Association for the Education of Young Children, June 1987), p. 15.
2. Marcy Whitebook, "The Teacher Shortage: A Professional Precipice," *Young Children*, March 1986, p. 11.
3. Willer, p. 8.
4. Nita Barbour and Don Pease, cochairpersons, Association for Childhood Education International Teacher Education Committee, "Preparation of Early Childhood Teachers," *Childhood Education*, May/June 1983, pp. 303-306.
5. National Association for the Education of Young Children, "Guidelines for Early Childhood Education Programs in Associate Degree Granting Institutions" (Washington, D.C.: NAEYC, 1985), pp. 4-5.
6. National Association for the Education of Young Children, "Early Childhood Teacher Education Guidelines for Four- and Five-Year Programs" (Washington, DC: NAEYC, 1982), pp. 2-3.
7. Lawrence J. Schweinhart, "When the Buck Stops Here: What It Takes to Run Good Early Childhood Programs," *High/Scope Resource*, Fall 1987, p. 10.
8. Joan Moyer, Harriet Egertson, and Joan Isenberg, "The Child-Centered Kindergarten," *Childhood Education*, April 1987, p. 240.
9. Mary Hatwood Futrell, "Public Schools and Four-Year-Olds: A Teacher's View" (Washington, D.C.: National Education Association, undated), p. 5.
10. Ellen Galinsky, "Promoting Positive Growth in Children Is No Accident," *Index: Child Care*, June 1987, p. 3.

The Importance of Parental Involvement

"It would be a national tragedy to waste current parental support for early childhood education, because that support can improve American student achievement more than all the school-reform proposals put together."
—Samuel G. Sava, Executive Director, National Association of Elementary School Principals

While the quality of the caregiver is central to program quality, the role of parents in preschool programs is also important, more so in programs for young children than in those for older youngsters. Parents, as their children's first educators, can help foster a bridge between home and early schooling experiences.

Many researchers have pointed to parental involvement as a key benefit to preschool programs.[1] The establishment of many more preschool programs will necessitate a shift toward the child care model of inviting parents to play an integral role in what may be their children's first out-of-home education and care experience.

High quality preschool programs therefore seek to involve parents not only in fund-raising and booster activities, but in policy making and planning. And those that enroll at-risk children are committed to strengthening families by offering support to parents.

BENEFITS TO ALL

The benefits of this involvement are numerous. Not only do parents gain a better view of the program itself, but they may develop a more thorough understanding of important child development issues. In this way, parents can help reinforce program goals at home by extending the learning that goes on in the classroom. And many parents who participate in programs develop more positive self-images and enroll in education or training programs themselves.

Caregivers benefit from parental involvement as well. They learn more about children's needs and environments by witnessing them with the people who are the major influences in their lives, and they can provide better links between the schooling experience and the home.

But perhaps most important is that children benefit. Research shows advanced cognitive development and academic achievement, better relationships at home, and increased feelings of security about home-school transitions.

EFFECTIVE COOPERATION

In encouraging parents to become part of their children's child care or school program, caregivers and teachers form with parents a partnership in the development of the children. Effective cooperation between parents and caregivers is vital to effective programs.

How, then, can parents be encouraged to take part in their child's preschool education? Consider the following suggestions from public school officials involved with successful preschool programs:

- "We don't sit in an ivory tower and plan in a vacuum, away from the parents," says Gloria Galey, administrator of the **Lubbock, Texas, Independent School District's** 15-year-old Developmental Education Birth-Through-Two project for handicapped children. "We survey parents, telephone them, have weekly phone visits with teachers, and have staff brainstorming." As a result, she says, "Our program has continued to change every year with changes in the population."
- In **Pendleton, Oregon's Umatilla Education Service District**, parents are made part of the individualized educational plan (IEP) developed for each child, says Ernest Cristler, Jr., special education director. Each IEP is in turn developed with a focus on parent needs. And the school works to link parents with other parents as a means of increasing communication and support.
- The policy committee of the **Ithaca City, New York, School**

District's Head Start program involves parents in program planning and goal setting. There are also home visits, classroom participation, legislative activities, and one-on-one discussions with families, says Prekindergarten Head Start Director Beverly Laforse.
- Superintendent Marvin Johnson of **Unified School District 413** in **Chanute, Kansas**, holds a kindergarten orientation tea to attract parents, and follows up with parent-teacher conferences twice yearly.

Written Communication

Regular, ongoing communication between parents and program staff is a must. Having a brochure or booklet to introduce parents and community members to program goals and other features is a real plus.

Have a program brochure

The **Delight, Arkansas,** Kiddieland Express Day Care Center parent information brochure welcomes children and parents and includes information on such topics as:
- Center goals.
- Policy on medicines and illnesses.
- Registration and fees.
- Admissions and attendance policies.
- Meals and snacks (what, when).
- Children's personal property (what's needed, what should be left at home, labeling).
- Curriculum.
- Hours of operation.
- Discipline policy.

Other districts have used booklets to address such issues as:
- Benefits for students, parents, community.
- Eligibility, enrollment.
- Funding sources, financial aid, scholarships.
- Conferencing procedures.
- Information on staff (who they are, their qualifications).
- Testing (what tests are given, when, what they measure).
- Group size, adult-child ratio.
- Policies on withdrawing children from the program.
- Transportation schedules.
- Explanations of screening and development.

When creating or adapting a written communication vehicle, consider including:
- A welcoming letter from the superintendent, board, or others.
- Schedule of several "typical" days.

- Location of message boards that contain information for parents.
- Schedule of the parent-advisory committee.
- Suggestions for parent involvement.
- Newspaper clips on the benefits of preschool programs.
- Telephone numbers of center administrators, directors.
- Calendar of the program year.
- Tips for preparing for the first day of the program.
- Information on learning at home.
- Community resources for parents (telephone numbers of social service agencies, for example).
- Definitions of various terms used in early childhood education.
- Updates on local, state, and national early childhood efforts, advocacy groups, and so forth.
- Names of publications, journals, books on early learning.

Publish a newsletter

Weekly or monthly newsletters to parents are also helpful, and regular parent conferences and workshops foster two-way communication.
- The **Grand Rapids, Michigan, public schools** publish a monthly newsletter for parents of children in its program for 3- to 5-year-olds. Included are notes from the staff, important dates, monthly learning activities and themes, an activity sheet, and a snack menu, according to Joanne Ayotte, administrator of elementary education.
- "We use extensive involvement of parents through written communication with monthly 'idea' sheets as well as practical 'make and take' workshops [at which parents can take away specific ideas for at-home development] held at night for parents," says T. Paul Vivian, Superintendent of **Florence County School District 2** in **Pamplico, South Carolina**, which offers a program for at-risk 4-year-olds.
- The staff of each school in the **Fairfax County, Virginia,** School-Age Child Care (SACC) program provides parents a newsletter every two weeks that includes important names and numbers; and special news about program events, staff, and students, goals and needs. On the back of the letter is a two-week schedule of activities arranged by age group and time of day. Fairfax extended-day program parents also receive a newsletter and other communiques from the SACC central administrative offices.

Daily Contact, Regular Participation

For some districts, daily contact with parents, whether by telephone or face-to-face, is essential for maintaining parent in-

SAMPLE CONTENTS OF LETTER TO PARENTS

What's Happening In Room 139

Dear Parents,

March has already come and gone. Before you know it, the school year will be over. Ms. Crenshaw and I have enjoyed getting to know you during our home visits.

We will start April off with Spring Vacation from March 28th–April 3rd. School will resume on Monday, April 4th. During the month of April, we will be doing and learning more exciting things. Our theme this month will center around Spring (signs of spring, weather, planting, etc.) and Land Transportation. Our readiness activities will include:

*Color: yellow (*April 26th, allow your child to wear something yellow)

Shape: circle

Number Concept: 1 and 2

Language: Same and Different, and continuation of individual learning goals.

April Birthdays
Happy Birthday to Joy Parker, April 13th, and Tracy Wilson, April 29th.

Mom's Day — For Mom's Only
All moms are invited to attend a special day at school with their child. We would like for moms to participate in an activity and share a snack with us. The morning class mom's day will be April 27th from 10:30 —11:20 a.m.; and the afternoon class will be from 2:10 —3:00 p.m. on April 28th. Invitations will be coming soon.

SOURCE: North Chicago Public Schools, Elementary School District 64, North Chicago, Ill.

volvement. Linda Kent, program development specialist for the **Lansing, Michigan, public schools,** says regular contact allows parents to understand their children's progress. In addition, individual conferences should be scheduled as needed or required.

Some preschool program administrators *require* parent participation, based on the belief that parent involvement is too important to leave to chance. This is the case in the **Hayward, California, Unified School District.** Officials there perform a needs assessment each fall and schedule evening meetings to address parent interests, according to Melinda Martin, director of early childhood education.

Here are other examples of how districts seek regular contact with parents:

- Parents whose children attend preschool programs at the **Independent, Wisconsin, public schools,** can take part in a parent-advisory council, a superintendent's roundtable, and a volunteer program, according to Superintendent Duane H. Sackett, who believes "some form of personal involvement" is important.
- For **El Paso Community Unit 375** in **El Paso, Illinois,** Friday is home visit day and school staff members call on parents to discuss the school program, children's development and progress, and related issues, according to Superintendent James Miller, whose district offers preschool programs for 3- to 5-year-olds.
- "The district has a coordinator for parent/community involvement," according to a **Pittsburgh, Pennsylvania,** Board of Education brochure. "Parent education sessions are held on a monthly basis. Several volunteer and involvement opportunities are provided. Parents are required to participate in a minimum of four hours parental involvement activities per month."

A number of states, mindful of the important link between parent involvement and school success, have instituted programs encouraging parent participation. Consider South Carolina's initiative: Through its Pages About Learning Skills (PALS) program, South Carolina identified 18 objectives to be addressed in all kindergarten programs. Among the objectives are: performing tasks involving gross and fine motor skills, remembering visual and auditory stimuli, and interpreting and inferring on the basis of oral or illustrative selections displaying a positive attitude toward school. Once the classroom teacher has addressed an objective, a PALS sheet is sent home suggesting activities to reinforce the objective. Parents are asked to practice the activities with their children for a maximum of 15 minutes three times weekly. Progress is recorded on the student's PALS record cards, which can be used in parent-teacher conferences.

Other ideas from successful programs:
- Send reports to parents detailing the objectives of the parent/teacher conferences to come (and summarizing those of the previous conference), and suggesting specific ways parents can reinforce what's being taught in school.
- Ask parents to volunteer in the classroom a certain number of times a year.
- Send home weekly child-parent homework sheets.
- Invite parents to inservice training programs.
- Create a parent library featuring resource materials.
- Offer parenting classes for new mothers and fathers.
- Involve parents of preschoolers through the school's parent-teacher organization; organize a parent group.

Program administrators also recommend the following:
- Initiate communication with parents early in the year, perhaps by publishing an orientation kit introducing parents to the program, explaining its goals, and outlining some major events.
- Schedule school meetings so that working parents can attend.
- Tell parents you *want* to hear their concerns and answer their questions.
- Conduct written and telephone surveys to determine parent needs and interests, then use responses to guide program development.
- Set up a "telephone tree" to enable important information to be communicated from one family to another as quickly as possible.
- Invite parents to visit the program at any time.

PARENTING SKILLS

Early childhood programs also involve and help parents by providing family support, from practical help in locating needed community resources to parent-education programs that offer information and discussion on such issues as child raising and development.

Two states have pioneered efforts in this area:
- **Missouri's Parents as Teachers project**. The first of its kind, this program is a home-school partnership designed to help parents give their children the best start and lay the foundation for later school success. Offered by all of Missouri's 543 school districts, the program provides early childhood screening and parent education for more than 35,000 families. Parents of children from birth to age three who take part in the program receive practical information about monitoring and fostering their children's early development. The result: Regardless of their

socioeconomic background, children of participating families were found to be significantly more advanced in language development than other 3-year-olds, according to an independent research study. They also made greater strides in problem-solving and other intellectual skills, advanced in social development, and demonstrated competencies predictive of and essential to school achievement.
- **Minnesota's Early Childhood Family Education programs.** Developed from 1974 to 1984, this program provides services to families with children from birth to the age of kindergarten enrollment. Emphasizing parent and family education, the program employs licensed parent educators and early childhood teachers who work directly with parents and children to offer discussion groups, workshops, and home visits. Also provided: early screening and detection of children's health and developmental problems; lending libraries of books, toys, and other learning materials; special events for the whole family; and information on community resources. Offered for free or for nominal fees by school districts with Community Education programs, ECFE is funded by a combined local levy/state aid formula that may be supplemented with registration fees and funds from other sources.

FAMILY SERVICES

Administrators of programs that enroll poor children should be aware of special non-educational needs—nutritional food, medical screening, literacy training, and job search assistance or training for parents—and seek to fill some of the gaps, either alone or cooperatively with community or state agencies. These services are based on the premise that healthy children come from healthy families, and represent a major component of programs like Head Start.

Consider a citywide, a district, and a local agency program:
- **New York City's Project Giant Step,** which is working to provide universal schooling for 4-year-olds, requires that programs have a social service component that includes regular contact by staff with social service agencies to develop programs and resources that address the needs of families and children. Project Giant Step staff must also conduct social service needs assessments for children and their families on a priority basis within 90 days of program entry; refer families to educational, legal, housing, counseling, crisis intervention, and other local social services; and provide outreach, crisis intervention, and individual counseling services, where possible.
- **Plainfield Public Schools** of **Central Village, Connecticut's**

REFUGEE FAMILIES...PROVIDING CULTURALLY SENSITIVE SERVICES

"Refugee" and "immigrant" are often used as interchangeable terms; however, significant differences in the definitions exist. Immigrants come to this country by choice and usually choose a destination for a job, for education, or to join family. They plan their departures and can maintain contact with those they left behind.

Refugees, on the other hand, are fleeing from a hostile government, are in precipitous flight, lose ties with the homeland and family, and do not know how long they will be in any place. They are at the mercy of other people.

During the fall of 1985, Spokane Head start was awarded a Head Start Innovative Grant to serve refugee infants, toddlers, and their parents in the eastern Washington city.

Through their efforts to provide comprehensive services, as well as classes in English as a Second Language, Spokane Head Start discovered that these families had multiple, complex problems that needed to be addressed. Their sense of identity and self worth were affected by the panic, shock, and trauma of their exodus. They experienced confusion with their new environments and language. They felt grief over the loss of their cultures.

The most obvious "obstacle" for the refugees was language. It was important to find translators who spoke the correct dialect, who were "trusted" figures, who were the appropriate sex and age (not children), and who could truly translate and not interpret or change meaning.

Through meetings with ethnic group leaders; reading relevant literature and attending training sessions; hiring bilingual staff; and sincerely acknowleding the importance of parents, Spokane Head Start administrators were able to develop culturally sensitive services.

For those involved in the program, it was encouraging to realize that through compassion and education they can and did make a difference.

SOURCE: Revised and reprinted from the National Head Start Bulletin, May 1989, Vol. 28, pp. 6, 11.

pre-school program for at-risk children and kindergarten, includes monthly home visits to seek parent involvement with program goals and objectives. Program staff also make referrals to other agencies when appropriate.
- **Family Focus Inc.'s West Town Center** in **Chicago** serves several hundred Hispanic families with children from birth to age 4. Parents receive support in various ways, ranging from English as a second language to training in health education and child development. Children are taken care of on a "drop-in" basis when their parents participate in center activities. The program is funded by foundations, corporations, and public agencies.

Schools offering part-day early childhood programs can help parents find affordable care to supplement their programs by inviting local providers into the school to address parents' needs and to answer questions. School officials can also provide transportation assistance by making school buses available for trips to and from local day care centers, and can work to coordinate schedules to minimize difficulties for children and parents taking advantage of a part-day program.

INVOLVING PARENTS IN THE TOTAL EDUCATIONAL SPECTRUM

The bottom line, in the words of Kevin Swick, professor of early childhood education at the University of South Carolina, is that "quality programs include parents in the total educational spectrum."[2] Special attention, Swick says, should be given to offering the services and support parents need to be effective with their children, especially for parents of at-risk children. And program administrators should work to develop a school setting where parents feel needed.

Toward this end, Superintendent Ronald McLeod, of the **El Paso Public Schools** in **El Paso, Texas,** advocates parent education for economically deprived and limited-English-speaking adults. "Those parents have the same aspirations as others, but do not have the knowledge of the bureaucracy that surrounds them. By teaching this component of the system, you will go a long way toward preventing potential dropouts."

Schools also should assess their parent-involvement efforts at regular intervals by asking parents—through home visits, telephone calls, or back-to-school nights—about their needs and suggestions for improvement.

Barriers to Involvement

Among the barriers that stand in the way of effective parent involvement efforts are:
- Parents who work full-time and may not have time for traditional school activities.
- Parents who prefer not to become involved.
- Parents with limited English proficiency.
- Teachers who do not welcome parent involvement. For example, teachers might resent having to spend additional time with parents who they may feel do not have the necessary training to participate in the classroom.

Progress in overcoming these problems can be made by educating parents and teachers about the crucial role of parents in their children's learning and development, by being flexible to such options as nighttime meetings, and by encouraging all those involved to adapt to changing times in light of the importance of their work. Providing special staff training in soliciting and managing parent involvement is also important.

Notes

1. Among the researchers and publications that have discussed the benefits of parental involvement to children and programs are: S.R. Andrews et. al., "The Skills of Mothering: A Study of Parent-Child Development Centers," *Monographs of the Society for Research in Child Development, 47,* (1982); H. Henderson, ed., *Parent Participation-Student Achievement: The Evidence Grows* (Columbia Md.: National Committee for Citizens in Education, 1981); and J. McKinney, *Evaluation of Parent Involvement in Early Childhood Programs 1979-1980* (Philadelphia, Pa.: Philadelphia School District, Office of Research and Evaluation, 1980).
2. Kevin J. Swick, "Involving Parents in Programs for Young Children," in Kevin J. Swick and Kathryn Castle, eds., *Acting on What We Know: Guidelines for Developing Effective Programs for Young Children* (Little Rock, Ark.: Southern Association on Children Under Six, 1985), p. 34.

7

Getting Started: How to Establish a Program

"At a time of rapid growth in early childhood programs, [school leaders] have a unique opportunity and responsibility to establish policies and practices that will ensure quality. This is a tremendous challenge, but one that can be met with effective leadership and an unyielding commitment to excellence in programs for young children."
—Barbara Day, professor and chair, and Tempe S. Thomas, research associate, University of North Carolina, School of Education, Division of Teaching and Learning, Chapel Hill[1]

For every school system with an interest in establishing an early childhood program, there is a different motivation. For some, parents' requests have brought the district to the point of pondering such a program. For others, awareness of the child care needs of working parents has led to the decision to implement a full-day kindergarten or an extended-day program for preschoolers. For still others, research on the effectiveness of early intervention has prompted them to design a program for at-risk children. The list goes on.

The procedures for developing an early childhood education program also differ considerably, based on the type of program offered, school location, school philosophy, level of commitment, community needs, and available funds. But most who establish new programs find it best to follow a basic procedure. And the first step in that procedure is conducting a needs assessment to determine current community programs and gaps that might be filled.

If the results of the assessment show the need for a program, the next step is forming a committee to study the specifics of establishing a program—taking into consideration such factors as legal requirements, regulation and licensing, funding, staff, eligibility, and curricula and materials.

Once the committee has completed its work and made recommendations, school officials must determine once again whether the school will provide the program prescribed. Sometimes, committees established to study the feasibility of offering early childhood programs find that funds or staff are insufficient at the current time and recommend against immediate start-up. Others will decide it is time to add the program and ask taxpayers to support it, while still others might develop some combination of ways to support the effort.

If the committee's recommendation is positive and the board acts to institute a program, launching the program is the next step. This stage should coincide with a vigorous public relations campaign to let parents and others in the community know all about the program.

STEP ONE: THE NEEDS ASSESSMENT

The object of conducting a needs assessment is to determine what types of early childhood and child care programs are currently provided in the community, what gaps are left unfilled, and what parents need and want in terms of child care and early childhood education.

Listen to the advice of administrators who have traveled this road:

- "Early childhood has recently become a focal point in education," notes Ann Foster, language arts and early childhood specialist in the **Fort Collins, Colorado, School District.** "It is essential that districts read, observe, assess, and understand all aspects of early childhood needs before initiating a program."
- Don't "plunge in without adequate research and study," notes Armand P. Premo, superintendent of the **Grand Isle Supervisory Union District** in **North Hero, Vermont.** And don't start "a program that is not well thought out in terms of program objectives."

Contact Existing Providers

In conducting a needs assessment, contact such potential early childhood and child care program sponsors as community organizations, churches and synagogues, individuals who run family day care homes, Head Start, and child care chains. Also look into programs offered through state health and social services agencies and through city and county government agencies.

The assessment should provide information on such areas as:
- How many children are served in how many programs?
- How many children remain on waiting lists to be admitted?
- The content and purpose of the programs.
- Program hours of operation and sponsorship.
- Cost and availability to parents.

At this stage, it is also wise to visit several different types of programs to view first-hand the ways early childhood programs differ in content, purpose, and organization. Visiting a variety of programs in the local area or elsewhere is also an excellent way to get an idea of how a new program, such as a school-based early intervention class, would fit in with the community's existing programs. Rather than looking at a school-based program as an option independent of other programs, consider how it might fit into the community's existing child care and early education framework, if one exists.

It may be appropriate, for example, to provide space for an after-school program staffed by the YWCA, or to offer school buses to a local Head Start program to facilitate transportation, as some schools currently do. Other schools find they can best fill a gap by supplementing existing half-day kindergarten programs with before- and after-school child care, so parents do not have to seek alternate arrangements for the remainder of the day.

Research Parents' Needs

The next step is to research the needs of area parents, both working and nonworking, to determine whether their needs are being met. Among questions to ask:
- Do parents want fast-paced academic programs, developmentally sound programs, or are they looking to schools to provide child care?
- Are there children in the community at risk of later school failure (children living in poverty, handicapped children, children for whom English is a second language, or latchkey children, for example) who are not being served?
- What additional programs are needed to serve these children and their parents?

- Can parents afford to pay for services? How much?

Note that if a survey is conducted, it should go beyond asking if families' child care and preschool needs are being fulfilled. Parents who have set up elaborate patchwork systems to ensure their children receive adequate care during the day, for example, might respond that their needs are met. But it is worth delving deeper to determine if those needs are met in a way satisfactory to the family, whether they are affordable, and whether parents consider them to be high in quality.

To perform this assessment, survey parents—all of them or a representative number, depending on the size of the community—directly through written or oral polls. Invite them to an assembly at the school or a local community center. Or ask local agencies to become involved in conducting a poll. Other sources to tap for information on parents' needs include local businesses, child care programs, local and county agencies that deal with children and families, and community groups familiar with the issue.

The survey also can help program planners determine whether parents would be interested in enrolling their children in a particular kind of program. But when this is done, it's important to make it clear that the school is only *considering* a program at this time. Making this clear will help avoid confusion should the decision be made not to begin a program.

Begin to Define the Program

Once the results of the needs assessment are in, it's time to determine whether an early childhood program is feasible. In a community in which child care and early intervention services are available and affordable to parents who need and want them, the decision may be no, as some school leaders have found. But in most communities, where needs are unmet and existing program costs are high, the school can fill an important void.

Many school administrators decide to appoint a committee made up of staff and community to consider in depth the elements that make up the program. But administrators who have implemented successful programs suggest that school officials discuss a general definition of the program *before* engaging a committee to hash out the details. By doing so, schools can present to committee members a framework for their work and discuss the basics of a sound program. Information is vital to good advice and good decisions.

In determining how best to fill that need, then, school leaders should develop a general idea, or list of options, of the program or programs the school would offer. For many communities, for example, the greatest need is for high quality, full-workday programs for 4-year-olds from low-income families. In any case, program deci-

POLICY ISSUES FOR STATES TO CONSIDER

Based on the results of a telephone survey conducted in 1986, Terry Gnezda and Susan Robinson of the National Conference of State Legislatures developed a list of policy considerations for state-funded prekindergarten early childhood education programs. Included in the survey were 16 states and the District of Columbia that have enacted state-funded preschool programs to provide educational experiences for young children.

Some of the policy issues determined by the survey results include:

- If the intent of early childhood education programs is to achieve the positive short- and long-term effects demonstrated in the research findings, state programs must reflect the high quality that was evident in the programs included in the research studies. Consideration of such components as teacher qualifications, low teacher-child ratios, small group size, and parental involvement is important.
- The timing of implementation is crucial to program success. Adequate lead time for planning and incorporation into the schools (or other settings) is essential. Securing adequate funding also is critical before implementation begins.
- To meet teacher shortages for early childhood education programs, alternatives to traditional certification procedures may be explored.
- It is important to consider effective integration of early childhood education programs into communities. The possibility of incorporating early childhood education programs into local child day care systems can be considered to address the child's educational needs and the parent's child care needs in an efficient and cost-effective way.

SOURCE: Reprinted with permission from "State Approaches to Early Childhood Education." Volume 11, No. 14, October 1986. Copyright © 1986 by the National Conference of State Legislatures, Denver, Colorado.

left off in considering the funding for an early childhood program: Will the existing budget be able to finance all or part of the program? If funding is low, will school leaders (particularly board members) support new funding? It may be necessary at this time to point out that preschool programs are a sound investment because they *prevent* problems in high-risk children. Thus, they save schools and the community the costs of working to correct problems later on.

In the search for funding, the committee also will want to research other sources:
- Meet with area superintendents who have successfully implemented similar programs and learn about their funding strategies.
- Ask state education department officials about available funds for new preschool programs.
- Tap local foundations with interest in education and children's issues.
- Write state legislators about the proposed program to learn if there are any initiatives under consideration.
- Work with local and state education and child advocacy groups to encourage funding for such programs.
- Talk to community child care providers to determine if there is interest in working with the schools to fill a child care need that would be less expensive than launching an independent program.

Once committee members have determined that there are enough funds to establish and operate a program, the committee should consider these related questions:
- How much money will be needed? How will the program be funded? Where will the money come from? What support will be provided by the state, local government, local businesses, parents, taxes, and other funding sources?
- Will the district charge a fee for parents who enroll their children in the program? Will it be a sliding-scale fee to take into account variations in income? Will scholarships or assistance be available for those who cannot afford the fee? If the program is geared to low-income children, what efforts will be made to ensure that all eligible children can participate?
- What kinds of insurance are needed (liability, health, accident, fire, building)? What parts of the program will be covered by existing school policy? How can insurance be obtained? How costly will it be?
- Will the program save the district any money (in transportation costs or by bringing tuition-paying students to now empty classrooms, for example)?

- How can possible changes in the program be anticipated —such as expansion of the number of children served? Can changes be worked into the funding equation?

Children (See Chapters 3 and 4)

In defining the program, the committee should determine what population of children will be served. It should also address a variety of issues related to enrollment; screening; assessment; class size and student-teacher ratio; and health, safety, and nutrition.

The committee will want to consider and make recommendations on the following issues:

- **Will the program be open to children in the district only or from other districts?** What about children of district employees?
- **Will the district test or screen children for eligibility or program entry?** What instruments will be used? Will there be other eligibility requirements? Will there be testing to determine post-program, pre-kindergarten, or first grade readiness? What measures will be taken to avoid inappropriate testing and mislabeling of children?
- **Will there be regular assessments of children?** Of what type? What standards will be set for observation and recording student progress and development?
- **How many children will be enrolled** in each class? Will there be minimum student-teacher ratios? Student-adult ratios?
- **What policy will be set for sick children**? Children with AIDS? How will the facility be adapted to accommodate children's needs? To ensure safety?

Teachers (See Chapter 5)

Committee members who have dealt with staffing considerations will find that there are similarities and differences in issues related to preschool staff. Since top-notch staff members are often cited as a key to high quality preschool programs, it is essential to consider this area carefully.

Among issues to deliberate:

- Will program teachers be required to have certain **credentials, child development training, experience?** This is one way administrators say they try to keep standards high; they also recommend hiring teachers who subscribe to program objectives and who *really* love working with preschool-age children.
- What role will **aides** play?
- How will the school **screen** to ensure new teachers do not have a history of child abuse? How will supervisors address re-

quirements to report suspected cases of abuse?
- How will **teachers' salaries** be determined? Will salaries be tied to existing school salary schedules or to local day care salaries, which are usually much lower? What about **benefits?** Compensation is one of the most difficult areas to address. Schools that pay early childhood or child care staff less than K-12 staff make a pretty clear statement that one is less important than the other. On the other hand, those who pay according to existing K-12 salaries may draw caregivers from lower-paying jobs to the schools and cause problems in the day care community. While it may be difficult to obtain funding for preschool teachers' salaries that is compatible with that of K-12 teachers, it is important to remember that better-paid preschool teachers stay in their jobs longer—resulting in less frequent turnover and overall benefit to the program.
- How will the program deal with the problems of **teacher turnover and burnout?** Will alternatives to traditional certification procedures be accepted?
- Who will provide **staff development?** How often? With what components? What efforts will be made to encourage collegiality, professional development, sharing of ideas? Will the district encourage teachers to attend conferences; will it provide funding or credits to do so?
- How will **administrators** be involved in the program? How will they provide continuing professional support for preschool teachers? How will teachers be involved in program development? Curriculum development? Policy planning? How will they interact with teachers at other grade levels?
- What is the program's policy for **teacher illness? Parental leave? Substitute teachers?**
- What policies will govern the **enrollment of teachers' children?** What about children of other school employees?
- Will the program hire **staff members other than teachers and aides,** such as social workers, cooks, nutritionists, parent liaisons, and so on?

Parents (See Chapter 6)

To a greater extent than in K-12 programs, parent involvement is a key component of high quality early childhood programs. Committee members, including parents, should address ways to invite parents to be an integral part of the preschool program, and to maintain their input and support.

Consider these issues:
- How will the program be structured to encourage regular and continuing **parental involvement?** To help facilitate involve-

ment for **working parents?**
- How will the program promote **home-school communication?** Make parents a larger part of their children's early childhood education?
- Will the program include a **parent education** component? Will it provide an outreach component to help parents of disadvantaged children taking part in the program?
- Will parents be encouraged to work in the planning of the program? Will they be encouraged to serve on **parent-advisory committees?**
- How will the program encourage **parents with concerns** about curriculum, their children's progress, or teachers to discuss their concerns to reach mutually satisfying conclusions?

Program Site and Components (See Chapters 3 and 4)

Making decisions about format, curriculum components, physical space, and the myriad issues raised in Chapter 3 is essential to a well-planned program.

Among the many issues that should be addressed are:
- What type of curriculum will be used? While the committee need not identify a specific curriculum model, it should define a curriculum plan or type so that goals and objectives can be outlined. Is it developmentally appropriate?
- How will the program address such components as play, language development, reading, computers, discipline?
- What kinds of materials (toys, books, outdoor equipment, etc.) will the program use?
- What meals and snacks will the program provide? Who will prepare them and where? How will the program incorporate nutritional information into the curriculum?
- Will medical services be provided? Screenings, check-ups, immunizations?
- In what ways will the program address multicultural issues and demonstrate sensitivity to children of all cultures?
- Where will the program be held? Is there on-site space available now or will space have to be found outside the school? How will existing or new space have to be modified to take into consideration the special needs of younger children, including safety and size considerations?
- Will the district provide transporation to children's homes or to community child care facilities if the school does not provide a full-work-day program?

The School and Community Framework

Once these questions have been addressed, committee members will need to consider how their responses and decisions affect the district's existing K-6 or K-12 program, the community, and families.

The establishment of new prekindergarten programs will have an effect on the early elementary grades. Most often, establishing a program for 4-year-olds will require changes to the district's kindergarten and first grade classes. A review of the early elementary grades' curricula and goals will need to be undertaken, in light of the proposed preschool program. The committee will want to research how children who participate in early childhood programs differ from those who do not take part in such programs in terms of school readiness, socialization skills, and other factors. In pondering the role of the preschool program in the total school framework, it must be recognized that schooling is a continuum and that each level reacts to change along the spectrum.

The committee will want to consider, too, how implementing a new program will affect existing early childhood and child care programs in the community, as well as the effect a new program will have on families' lives.

Among questions to discuss:
- How will the district's program affect children who move to other districts or states without similar programs?
- Will the establishment of a preschool program affect other area schools?
- If the school provides a part-day program, will it make facilities available to local child care providers or programs to offer child care for the remainder of the day?

Troubleshooting

Finally, the committee should consider the obstacles that are likely to stand in the way of effective program implementation. To identify likely obstacles, discuss implementation with administrators who have set up programs, with child care providers who offer programs to the community, with parents who raise possible objections, and with others. Also, conduct a careful review of the related research.

It's far better to overcome potential obstacles with a committee before instituting a program, say those with experience in the field, than to have to overcome hurdles as a program supervisor once the program is in place.

Maintaining a High Quality Program

"In order to maintain the quality of any child care arrangement, there needs to be a continual process of stock taking. Good child care is in a constant state of evolution. The caregivers are open to new ideas as they stay in touch with and respond to their own needs as well as the needs of the children and families they serve."
—Ellen Galinsky, president of the National Association for the Education of Young Children and director of Work and Family Life Studies at Bank Street College of Education

Once a high quality early childhood program is in place, program administrators must pay attention to the essentials of maintaining the quality of that program. Among them: a recognition of the importance of day-to-day matters, of regular evaluation, and of the benefits of acting on the results of evaluation.

To maintain quality, a preschool program—like any other educational program—must be monitored continually to ensure it meets the standards and goals established for its success. And because programs for young children are best when they are flexible and fluid, it is important to be open to change and encourage it on a regular basis.

Observation and discussion of daily issues and concerns by teachers, other school staff, parents, and community members are also important to maintaining a good preschool program. In addition to being aware of internal issues, program administrators will need to keep abreast of changes in federal, state, and local regulations; changes in funding or conditions of funding; variations in the population of the community; and new developments in the community, as well as in the early childhood field as a whole.

DAY-TO-DAY MANAGEMENT

Most public school administrators of early childhood and child care programs know how to manage programs based on their K-12 experiences. Essentially, being an effective manager of a preschool program is similar to running a good elementary school program; but there are some differences.

Because staff quality is closely tied to preschool program quality, it is essential that a district not only hire top teachers, aides, and other adults, but that it monitor and ensure the quality of staff on an ongoing basis. Regular inservice training sessions help in this area, as do regular sessions to encourage teacher and staff input.

"Sending them to courses once a semester won't do it," says Roger Neugebauer, editor of *Child Care Information Exchange* and an expert on program management. More effective, he advises, are monthly meetings focused on areas in which caregivers are weakest, including communicating with children and classroom management. Acting out situations, providing background information on the importance of an issue, and giving teachers specific ideas to use the following week can help ensure that gaps in program quality are addressed, says Neugebauer.

In addition, program administrators will want to embrace an attitude toward parents that may be different from the way they view parents of K-12 students. Procedures should be developed that prompt teachers to talk with parents weekly about their children's development and needs. To encourage this, Neugebauer says, it may be helpful for program staff to think of parents "as the people who sign [teachers'] paychecks."[1]

Other ideas for maintaining day-to-day quality:
- Foster relationships with the community's child care leaders, including local and state professional groups and local university child development departments. Maintain ongoing communication to increase the exchange of ideas and learn about new developments.
- Encourage staff members to meet regularly to discuss goals, problems, concerns, areas for improvement, and ideas.
- Make early childhood development literature available to teachers and other staff members (see the appendices in this book for sources).

> # BARBARA DAY ON SUPPORTING EARLY CHILDHOOD PROGRAMS DAILY
>
> *Barbara Day is professor and chair of the Department of Teaching and Learning in the School of Education at the University of North Carolina at Chapel Hill.*
>
> "I find that most teachers are very open to doing whatever they think will be helpful for the children in their classrooms. Most teachers really do trust and respect children; they support a child-centered philosophy that stresses peer interaction, learning by doing, and positive self-concept development.
>
> The problem comes with the support they need, financial and moral. To have a developmental classroom, you must have a wide variety of concrete and sensory materials. The classroom needs to be organized with experiential learning centers that allow for differences in learning styles, that encourage children to explore a variety of materials and make decisions.
>
> "A principal or administrator must believe that this kind of experiential learning is the way children grow, and must reward teachers through his or her comments, through his or her endorsement of materials they need and want, and through saying to the community, 'We have a fine program here.'"
>
> SOURCE: Ronald S. Brandt, "On Early Education: A Conversation with Barbara Day," *Educational Leadership* (November 1986): pp. 28-30. Reprinted with permission of the Association for Supervision and Curriculum Development and Barbara Day.

- Share ideas with administrators of other district preschool programs. Provide teachers opportunities to meet with preschool staff from other districts, as well.
- Get involved in local, state, and national associations that serve as information exhange and staff development centers.

Consistent Funding a Necessity

Administration support of teachers goes a long way toward ensuring maintenance of quality staff. Also important to the daily operation of a high-quality program is a continued commitment to funding. Consistent funding translates into higher morale and allows program staff to concentrate on the important issues of child development instead of having to turn their attention to seeking ongoing support.

To keep funding constant, it's essential to tell the community about the program on a regular basis:
- Invite board members and other school officials to visit classrooms.
- Hold an open house for local businesses.
- Videotape classes to show at meetings of community leaders and groups.
- Continually publicize information about the program and its successes in the news media and in district publications.
- Accept all opportunities to talk about the program.

It may also be wise to refrain from disbanding the committee that worked to form the program. A committee with the power to recommend changes is an important asset, notes an administrator whose school offers Head Start, Chapter 1 preschool, special education, and transitional first-grade programs. The committee can meet monthly to address such issues as ongoing funding support, teacher inservice development, changing curriculum goals, and parent input. It can also help devise evaluation instruments. Members can be appointed for one- or two-year terms.

The committee, or the program director, should plan regular presentations to the board (or other funding source) on the program's progress. Ongoing board support is important, and program administrators who have had success in this area stress the following practices:
- In regular memos to board members, administrators should keep them informed about the program, says James Walker, Jr., director of program services for **North Chicago District 64 in Illinois.**
- Encourage satisfied parents to convey their support to the board. "It isn't easy [to maintain support] at the local level," says Marilyn Edgar, principal of the **Pinckney, Michigan, community schools.** "Parents with children in the program are the best advocates."
- Ensure that board members "are kept informed of the issues and research in support of early childhood education and child care," advises Linda Kent, program development specialist for the **Lansing, Michigan, public schools.**

The Benefits of Regular Evaluation

Children who participate in preschool programs that are not of high quality do not reap the same benefits as those who take part in high quality programs, according to the research. For a program to be effective, then, its quality must be maintained. That is the administrator, principal, board, or others) evaluate staff at least annually, focusing on classroom observation based on criteria that have been discussed with the teacher or caregiver in advance. Results, which are written and confidential, should be discussed privately with each staff member; and staff should be given opportunities to evaluate their own performance. The process naturally leads to new ideas for improved staff training.

Acting on the Results

Evaluating a program is just the first step toward assuring high quality. The next and, perhaps, the most crucial step is translating the results of that evaluation into change—improvements that make the program the best it can be.

If the team conducting the evaluation has made specific recommendations, those recommendations should be reviewed and discussed with staff and reviewed by board members or other governing or funding sources. If specific suggestions have not been made, it is up to program administrators and staff to determine how to translate evaluation results into improvements.

Once needed improvements are agreed upon, program staff should set and maintain a schedule for making changes. Regular checks will have to be made to ensure that the changes have been implemented well, are producing the desired results, and have not led to other problems. Again, constant fine-tuning is the best way to run a high quality early childhood program. Acceptance of a state of constant flux is important because young children change daily, and all adults associated with the program should be flexible enough to adapt their methods and components of the program to meet children's needs.

Finally, program administrators and staff should keep Epstein's advice in mind: "Good evaluations make intuitive sense...They ask meaningful questions and answer them in logical ways. Trust your own intuition. No one knows a program better than the staff involved in its day-to-day operation."[5]

Knowing the early childhood program inside and out, program administrators and staff are in the best position to effect the changes needed to maintain high quality and ensure the best programs for young children.

Notes

1. For more information on day-to-day management of early childhood programs, see *Child Care Information Exchange,*, published monthly by Roger and Bonnie Neugebauer (Exchange, P.O. Box 2890, Redmond, WA 98073-2890).
2. Lawrence J. Schweinhart, *A School Administrator's Guide to Early Childhood Programs* (Ypsilanti, Mich.: High/Scope Press, 1988), pp. 35-36.
3. Lawrence J. Schweinhart and Elizabeth Mazur, "Prekindergarten Programs in Urban Schools" (Ypsilanti, Mich.: High/Scope Educational Research Foundation, in collaboration with the Council of Great City Schools, 1987), p. 19.
4. Ann Epstein, "A No-Frills Approach to Program Evaluation," *High/Scope ReSource*, Winter 1988, p. 12.
5. Epstein, p. 12.

private, nonsectarian and sectarian, and public funding should be available to these different providers, provided that religious instruction is not publicly funded. To date, nursery schools and other prekindergarten and early childhood education programs have developed primarily under private auspices. Head Start programs have been established successfully in a variety of locations—community-based organizations, private facilities, and in public schools. And there is an increasing number of state and locally funded pre-K programs in schools, especially for 4-year-olds. Having multiple sources provides alternatives, a healthy competition at this level of education, and a variety of approaches from which families may select.

To ensure multiple providers without isolating children by economic standing, the federal government will need to develop the Head Start program so that it serves all eligible children. It also will need to sponsor a new initiative that will expand early childhood education programs in public schools, as well as expand service in the private schools and authorize contracts with other providers.

3. **Funding for prekindergarten education should be mixed** with 1) assistance coming from federal, state, and local levels of government and 2) funding provided through both public and private resources with authority for the charge of sliding scale fees for those families that can afford services. Funding, in fact, should be more akin to the patterns of support for postsecondary education than is currently the case for elementary and secondary education. It should be primarily to institutional providers rather than to individuals. Because prekindergarten is not compulsory, certain ground rules that relate to financing of public elementary and secondary education need not apply.

4. **Public funding from federal, state, and local sources should be carefully integrated so that there is an obligation for continuing support for all levels of government.** Such integration will be most effectively provided where federal funds are linked with primary sources of elementary and secondary school support, namely local tax levy and state resources for elementary and secondary education. Key leverage points will be realized if federal funds are so connected.

5. **The structure of authority and governance for prekindergarten education should be more directly related with the structure of governance for elementary and secondary education.** New or expanded responsibilities should be established within the existent structure of local boards of education and state boards of education; this being preferable to creating a new, elaborate local and state machinery.

6. **Early childhood education, child care, and health services must be seen as complimentary and not competing.** Prekindergarten programs will in all likelihood not be provided on a full-day or even a full-school-day basis. It's essential that these programs be linked with child care, which assures the child has a full-day program related to parents' work schedule.

   The primary means for assuring this would be to link the provisions for early childhood education, child care, and health services together in the same bill before the U.S. Congress, so that they are not passed at different times and do not appear to be competing in different ways for appropriations.
7. **Prekindergarten programs must have a strong parent and family component.** This component should not only elicit the participation of the parent and family in support of the child's activity, but also assist the parent and family in strengthening its capacity as "educator."

RECOMMENDATIONS FOR ACTION

Public schools that choose to establish early childhood programs, and all those interested in the opportunities such programs represent for children, families, and society as a whole, must seriously evaluate all proposals for meeting the ever-increasing need for early childhood care and education, and then work to effect changes on the local, state, and national/federal levels. Here are a few specific recommendations:

Local Level

- **Start small and start smart.** Avoid the temptation to simply copy what the neighboring district is doing or follow what national leaders recommend just because it's trendy or makes headlines. Instead, study your district's needs and look at what's already being provided. Determine whether parents' interest in early schooling is really a call for affordable and available child care. Investigate funding sources before committing yourself to program development. Then, if you do decide to begin a program, start a pilot project with a definite time-line and evaluation component to determine how best to provide the needed services.
- **Work with the people who know young children well.** Meet with parents, child development experts, academicians who have researched the field, and local child care providers with an eye toward merging resources. Learn from their experience. Work

together to avoid duplicating services and to provide excellent programs for children.

- **Make parents primary partners in the preschool experience.** Recognize the essential role parents play as their children's first teachers. Understand the importance of working with them on a continual basis to help in the development of children and meet parents' needs as well. Offer parenting skills classes for adults and child development classes for high school students. As well, be sensitive to the cultural differences in families, and recognize the desire and abilities of families to help their children.
- **Recognize the needs of children and families in poverty.** Understand the importance of serving all children. Design programs, such as full-workday developmental care, to meet some of the needs of low-income parents. Work with other local agencies, such as community groups that operate Head Start programs, to coordinate responses to meet the needs of poor families whose children attend public school. Make sure all children can continue to attend programs by ensuring adequate program funding.
- **Hire staff members who are trained, experienced, and love working with young children.** Then pay them well to show the importance of their work in children's development, encourage respect of those who work in the field, and help lessen the damaging effects of turnover.
- **Provide staff with regular opportunities for inservice training.** Expose them to new ideas, encourage them to read pertinent literature, introduce them to others in the field. Be sure they're involved in professional organizations and activities. Support early childhood teachers' work on a regular basis.
- **Establish ties with local businesses and other organizations to further child development programs.** Consider working with local firms, community organizations, or existing child care providers to provide preschool or extended-day programs on school premises. Enter into partnerships with individuals or groups interested in giving support to child care programs, health services, and social programs for low-income parents. Make space available and offer school expertise.
- **Monitor the changing characteristics of your community.** Conduct periodic surveys—formal or informal—to determine how your community is changing. Keep abreast of the numbers of working parents, the economic factors affecting your district, changes in the types of families, and new needs that arise as a result of these changes.
- **Ensure that programs are developmentally appropriate.** Learn more about how young children learn and develop. Make sure your program reflects that knowledge. Steer clear of a traditional K-12 academic approach.

- **Structure programs so that they enable children to make a smooth transition into elementary school.** Provide program experiences that integrate well with the patterns and scheduling of more formal schooling.
- **Ensure that all early childhood education is well integrated.** Re-evaluate kindergarten- through third-grade offerings in light of preschool and pre-K programs and make necessary changes to ensure alignment of learning components.
- **Establish programs that will help each child develop a full range of abilities.** These abilities should be social, emotional, physical, and cognitive; taking into account the developmental differences of each child.

State Level

- **Encourage cooperation among state agencies.** Consider, for example, Minnesota's interagency agreement on early childhood intervention. In 1984, the state's departments of education, health, and human services signed an agreement to promote the development of coordinated multidisciplinary systems for serving handicapped children and children at risk of handicapping conditions, from birth through age five, and their families. Such cooperation is essential to providing high quality programs. It encourages groups to work together for the benefit of children, sharing experience and information. It also helps avoid overlapping services, turf-guarding, and splintering of funds.
- **Promote state legislation to revise teacher certification requirements.** Revisions should include more emphasis on training, courses, and field experience appropriate to those working with young children. Legislation could also address requirements for continued inservice training at the district level. If a teacher shortage exists, alternatives to certification may need to be explored, or salaries and promotion may have to be increased.
- Encourage teacher, administratror, parental, community, and business innovation through recognition programs. One example would be an award that recognizes creative ways teachers involve parents in the early childhood program.
- Provide technical assistance. For example, states could establish a clearinghouse for information on available early childhood and child care programs, train individuals to set up parent groups to get them more involved, or set up parent centers in different parts of the state where parents could participate in workshops or obtain parenting skills materials.
- Support model and demonstration programs. These programs enable school districts to envision what is possible in the way of early childhood education and child care. If state funds are not

ONLY IF...

Many state legislatures are considering bills that could add local and state resources to child care and early education programs. However, this enhanced role for the school system will have positive effects only if certain conditions are spelled out in the legislation for these early childhood programs. Funds should be available for early education through the school system only if:

- This money adds to the total resources for child care and early education programs. *Not* if legislators simply shift or reduce funding from Head Start and the social service system to support school-based programs.
- Schools can choose to institute such programs. *Not* if schools lacking interest in early childhood programs are mandated to start them.
- Early childhood experts are involved in planning with the schools. *Not* if schools initiate early childhood programs without input from those in the community who know about child development and early education.
- The needs of kindergarten children are addressed as well. *Not* if schools with low-quality kindergarten programs are required to add four-year-old programs without also upgrading their kindergarten program.
- The schools are required to have a plan to make four-year-old programs accessible to all children, with parent fees on a sliding scale, if necessary. *Not* if school-based programs serve only certain children based on income, social class, or race.
- Provisions ensure that the needs of children of full-time employed parents are met by the addition of school-based early childhood programs. *Not* if these programs are likely to increase the number of latchkey children in the community.
- Parents would be welcome and respected as partners in early childhood programs for their children. *Not* if the orientation is to ignore both parent input and children's family and cultural heritage.

SOURCE: Revised from Gwen Morgan, "Child Care and Early Education: What Legislators Can Do," in *Programs for Four-year-Olds* resource guide (Washington, D.C.: National Association for the Education of Young Children, 1986).

sufficient, states can solicit private funds.
- Facilitate training. Another way states can facilitate better school/family relationships is to provide inservice and preservice training for teachers and administrators to instruct them on how to work with different types of families, and training programs for students and interested adults to help them learn how to work with young children in the schools. Selected teachers could receive additional training so they can become specialists in family involvement and strengthen relationships between home and school.

National Level

- **Promote federal legislation and funding for early childhood programs.** Though federal aid would be beneficial to the entire scope of services to families and children, ranging from infant care and after-school programs to parental education and training, one of the most helpful actions the federal government could take would be to increase its funding for both Chapter 1 and Head Start. Though Smart Start, a 1988-89 proposed program to serve 4-year-olds, is laudable, it is imperative that children at risk—including those in economic need — be adequately served.
- **Urge senators and congressmen to develop legislation that would encompass the best ideas from existing federal programs.** Any approach should take into account the need for full funding of Chapter 1 and Head Start. Funds for these areas should be targeted for both program and inflationary growth.

Local, State, and National Levels

- **Work to uncover new funding for children's programs.** If financial reasons are what's preventing schools from starting a program for which there is community need, work for more funding instead of giving up. Talk to people who have uncovered innovative funding ideas. Work with local, state, and national associations to communicate with state and local boards of education, state legislatures, and Congress about the need for additional monies. Join with corporations and private providers to develop lower-cost alternatives to traditional methods.
- **Continue to work to meet the overall needs of children, even after a local program is established.** Work with local and state organizations to address the need for increased funding. Underscore the importance of high quality by keeping up with and widely distributing research results. Maintain local standards that ensure quality. Become a lifelong advocate for children.

- **Work with the media to gain and further support.** Build public advocacy efforts for early childhood education and child care by working with the media. Maintain regular contacts with local and state newspaper, radio, and television representatives. Communicate the message that society's children are our nation's future.
- **Advocate a district-to-national-level discussion of early childhood education.** Talk to local, state, and national groups representing public school teachers, administrators, principals, and parents, plus associations representing child care workers, private providers, pediatricians, state legislators, Head Start workers, researchers, employers, and others. Encourage them to meet to discuss the issues of appropriate services, sponsorship, child care needs, research and its implications, and funding. Among the potential results of such a meeting (or series of meetings): an understanding of each player's needs and interests; a recognition of how to promote and obtain funding from states and the federal government; a discussion of how best to encourage the public schools—in many cases a new player in the field—to provide services in cooperation, not competition, with existing providers; a plan for dissemminating this type of information to all involved on the local level in program development and operation; and, perhaps most important, an understanding of what's best for children.

Richard Wallace, Superintendent of the **Pittsburgh, Pennsylvania, School District,** emphasizes the importance of public schools working in harmony with existing agencies. "The wave of the future in education has got to include dealing with programs for 3- to 5-year-olds, both by public schools and public schools in collaboration with existing early childhood programs. We cannot rob them (existing early childhood agencies) of what they have been doing on that."

"Early childhood professionals and advocates must become equal partners with schools and legislators when decisions are made affecting young children," recommends Helen Blank, director of child care at the Children's Defense Fund. Early childhood representatives, she says, should take an active role in shaping programs and policy. "We can help others recognize the components of high quality, appropriate, and comprehensive programs for young children."[2]

Notes

1. Marvin Cetron, et. al., *Schools of the Future* (New York: McGraw-Hill Book Company, 1985), pp. 68, 70, 80.
2. Helen Blank, "Early Childhood and the Public Schools: An Essential Partnership," *Young Children*, May 1985, pp. 54- 55.

Appendix I

Organizations Active in Early Childhood Education and Child Care

The following list includes the names, addresses, and telephone numbers of organizations, groups, and agencies that work in the early childhood education and child care fields. Also included is a brief description of each organization and the work it is doing in the field. As well, the efforts of some of these organizations are described in depth in Chapter 1.

Alliance for Better Child Care
c/o Helen Blank
Children's Defense Fund
122 C St. N.W.
Washington, DC 20001
(202) 628-8787

OR

c/o Barbara Reisman
Child Care Action Campaign
99 Hudson St.
New York, NY 10013
(212) 334-9595

ABC is a coalition of more than 70 national organizations formed to develop legislation to create a national child care policy and a federal investment in the children of America's working parents.

American Academy of Pediatrics
141 Northwest Point Road
P.O. Box 927
Elk Grove, IL 60007
(800) 433-9016

The AAP, an organization of more than 29,000 board-certified pediatricians, recently joined with several education associations to work on behalf of developmentally appropriate early educational experiences for children.

American Association of School Administrators
1801 North Moore St.
Arlington, VA 22209-9988
(703) 528-0700

AASA, a professional organization for more than 18,500 education leaders, supports policies and practices that will make it possible for all children, including the disadvantaged, to receive the services of their schools at an early age. Such programs should be developmentally appropriate, should not rush children, and should feature parenting education, where possible.

American Federation of Teachers
555 New Jersey Ave. N.W.
Washington, DC 20001
(202) 879-4400

The AFT, which represents 620,000 teachers, has since the 1970s supported public-school sponsorship of early childhood education programs.

Association for Childhood Education International
11141 Georgia Ave., Suite 200
Wheaton, MD 20902
(301) 942-2443

ACEI, a membership organization with members from 50 states and 20 countries worldwide, is concerned with issues related to children from infancy through early adolescence.

Association for Supervision and Curriculum Development
125 North West St.
Alexandria, VA 22314
(703) 549-9110

A 72,000-member association, the ASCD is studying the issue of the school's role in the education and care of young children.

Association of Child Advocates
P.O. Box 5873
Cleveland, OH 44101-0873
(216) 881-2225

ACA is a national association of independent, state-based child-advocacy organizations. Founded in 1984, it is concerned about the healthy growth of America's children and works to strengthen and encourage the development of advocacy organizations.

Bank Street College of Education
610 West 112th St.
New York, NY 10025
(212) 663-7200
(see School Age Child Care Project)

Carnegie Foundation for the Advancement of Teaching
1755 Massachusetts Ave. N.W.
Washington, DC 20036
(202) 387-7200

The Foundation is studying children from birth to age four, as well as children in the early elementary years. The findings will be released in a two-part report that will be available in 1991.

Child Care Action Campaign
99 Hudson St., Room 1233
New York, NY 10013
(212) 334-9595

This is a national advocacy coalition, founded in 1983, that provides information and resources on child care issues of importance to the nation.

Child Care Employee Project (CCEP)
P.O. Box 5603
Berkeley, CA 94705
(415) 653-9889

This non-profit advocacy organization conducted the National Child Care Staffing Study, which provided national data on characteristics of child care providers linked to measures of child care quality. The organization works to improve the wages, status, and working conditions of the child care profession.

Child Care Law Center
625 Market St., Suite 816
San Francisco, CA 94105
(415) 495-5498

The Center researches and disseminates information on all areas of child care and offers more than 50 brief publications dealing with legal issues such as liability, taxes, zoning, and child abuse.

Children's Defense Fund
122 C St. N.W.
Washington, DC 20001
(202) 628-8787

The CDF is a children's advocacy organization dedicated to improving the welfare of children. It works actively in the field of child care: disseminating information, lobbying, and publishing materials.

Child Welfare League of America
444 First St. N.W., Suite 520
Washington, DC 20001
(202) 638-2952

The Child Welfare League lobbies and advocates on issues related to child welfare.

The Children's Foundation
815 15th St. N.W., Suite 928
Washington, DC 20005
(202) 347-3300

The Children's Foundation is a national organization that advocates for women and children on social and economic issues. The Foundation sponsors the National Family Day Care Project, which provides technical assistance and professional support to organizations and providers.

The Conference Board
845 Third Ave.
New York, NY 10022
(212) 759-0900
The Conference Board is a not-for-profit business research organization. Its Work and Family Information Center addresses, among others, issues related to families and children.

Education Commission of the States
1860 Lincoln Ave., Suite 300
Denver, CO 80295
(303) 830-3600
Created to help state leaders improve the quality of education, ECS provides state-level information on education, and has published such material as a 50-state survey of state action in early childhood education for 3-, 4-, and 5-year-olds.

ERIC Clearinghouse on Elementary and Early Childhood Education
College of Education, University of Illinois
805 West Pennsylvania Ave.
Urbana, IL 61801-4897
(217) 333-1386
Through ERIC, a nationwide information system funded by the Office of Educational Research and Improvement, the clearinghouse provides information on early childhood education and the elementary grades—including child development, parenting, learning, teacher preparation, and programs. Among its services: *ERIC Digests*, annotated resource lists, publications, and searches.

Family Resource Coalition
230 North Michigan Ave., Suite 1625
Chicago, IL 60601
(312) 726-4750
A national federation of more than 2,000 individuals and organizations, the Family Resource Coalition is devoted to promoting the development of prevention-oriented, community-based programs to strengthen families.

Head Start Bureau
Administration for Children, Youth, and Families
U.S. Department of Health and Human Services
P.O. Box 1182
Washington, DC 20013
(202) 755-7762
The Head Start Bureau administers the 22-year-old Project Head Start, the government's largest commitment to disadvantaged preschool children in full- and part-day programs.

High/Scope Educational Research Foundation
600 North River St.
Ypsilanti, MI 48197
(313) 485-2000
High/Scope, perhaps best known for its work on the Perry Preschool

Project, is a research institution dedicated to addressing a wide variety of issues related to early childhood education, including at-risk children, teacher training, and state legislation.

Infant Care Leave Project
Bush Center in Child Development and Social Policy
P.O. Box 11A Yale Station
Yale University
New Haven, CT 06520
(203) 436-1921

The Infant Care Leave Project conducted a series of studies designed to assess current knowledge on issues affecting working families with infants; a compilation of the material was published in 1987. The Project also convened an advisory committee on infant care leave.

National Academy of Early Childhood Programs
(see National Association for the Education of Young Children)

National Association for the Education of Young Children
1834 Connecticut Ave. N.W.
Washington, DC 20009
(202) 232-8777

NAEYC, an organization representing 54,000 educators, policy makers, researchers, practitioners, and parents, works on behalf of early childhood educators. NAEYC also administers the National Academy of Early Childhood Programs, the only national, voluntary accreditation program for early childhood programs and child care centers.

National Association for Family Day Care
5153 Gramercy Drive
Clifton Heights, PA 19018
(215) 622-0663

NAFDC deals with issues related to family day care.

National Association of Early Childhood Specialists in State Departments of Education
c/o Harriet A. Egertson
Early Childhood/Elementary Education
Nebraska Department of Education
301 Centennial Mall South
Lincoln, NE 68509
(402) 471-2444

NAECS/SDE is a national organization for state education agency staff with major responsibility in early childhood education. Members work to enhance department efforts on behalf of young children, strengthen communication and coordination among states, and influence and support policies and legislation.

National Association of Elementary School Principals
1615 Duke St.
Alexandria, VA 22314
(703) 684-3345

Representing 23,000 elementary-school principals, NAESP is developing guidelines for implementing programs for 4- and 5-year-olds; holding regional workshops (with High/Scope) on training principals; working with state affiliates to help develop legislation; and collaborating with a number of associations in the field of early childhood education.

National Association of State Boards of Education
700 N. Fairfax St., Suite 340
Alexandria, VA 22314
(703) 684-4000
NASBE, a nonprofit association serving state boards of education, recently formed a task force on early childhood education to develop a new vision for the role of schools in prekindergarten programs.

National Association of State Directors of Child Development
c/o Marian Monroe
Child Development Program Director
Family Support Resources Division
Texas Department of Human Services
John H. Winters Human Services Center
701 West 51st St.
P.O. Box 2960, M.C. 523-E
Austin, TX 78769
(512) 450-4167
NASDCD, established in the 1970s with the support and assistance of the U.S. Department of Health and Human Services, exchanges state reports, examines existing and proposed federal legislation, and serves as a consultant to federal, state, and private agencies.

National Black Child Development Institute
1463 Rhode Island Ave. N.W.
Washington, DC 20005
(202) 387-1281
NBCDI is a nonprofit, national charitable and educational organization dedicated to improving the quality of life for black children. Founded in 1970, it focuses on the policy issues of child care, child welfare, and education.

National Center for Clinical Infant Programs
733 15th St. N.W., Suite 912
Washington, DC 20005
(202) 347-0308
NCCIP is a nonprofit organization established by lay and professional leaders in mental health, pediatrics, and child development. Through its work, the Center aims to improve and support professional initiatives in infant health, mental health, and development.

National Conference of State Legislatures
1050 17th St., Room 2100
Denver, CO 80265
(303) 623-7800
NCSL provides issue briefs and legislators' guides on issues including education, and answers information requests from across the country.

Halpern, Robert, "Major Social and Demographic Trends Affecting Young Families: Implications for Early Childhood Care and Education," *Young Children*, September 1987.

McCartney, K., et. al., "Environmental Differences Among Day Care Centers and Their Effects on Children's Development," in Zigler, E.F., and E.W. Gordon, eds., *Day Care: Scientific and Social Policy Issues* (Boston: Auburn House, 1982).

McKey, R.H., et. al., "The Impact of Head Start on Children, Families, and Communities, Final Report of the Head Start Evaluation, Synthesis, and Utilization Project" (Washington, D.C.: CSR Incorporated for the Head Start Bureau, Administration for Children, Youth, and Families, U.S. Department of Health and Human Services, 1985).

Petty, Walter T., and Robert J. Starkey, "Oral Language and Personal and Social Development," in Walter T. Petty, ed., *Research in Oral Language Development* (Champaign, Ill. National Council of Teachers of English, 1967).

Ramey, C., and Haskins, R., "The Causes and Treatment of School Failure: Insights from the Carolina Abecedarian Project," in M.J. Begab, H.C. Haywood, and H.L. Garter, eds., *Psychological Influences in Retarded Performance: Strategies for Improving Competence* (Baltimore, Md.: University Park Press, 1981).

Rohe, W., and A. Patterson, "The Effects of Varied Levels of Resources and Density on Behavior in a Day Care Center," in D.H. Carson, ed., *Man-Environment Interactions* (Washington, D.C.: EDRA, 1974).

Ruopp, R., et. al., "Children at the Center: Final Report of the National Day Care Study" (Cambridge, Mass.: Abt Associates, 1979).

Schweinhart, Lawrence J., and David P. Weikart, eds., "The Perry Preschool Program and Its Long-Term Effects: A Benefit Cost Analysis," Early Childhood Policy Paper No. 2 (Ypsilanti, Mich.: High/Scope Educational Research Foundation, 1985).

Public-School Sponsorship of Early Childhood Programs

Blank, Helen, "Early Childhood and the Public Schools: An Essential Partnership," public policy report, *Young Children*, May 1985.

"Child Care and the Role of the Public Schools," report of December 10-12, 1984, conference in Wyzata, Minn. (ERIC Document 264 013).

"Child Care in the Public Schools: Incubator for Inequality?" (Washington, D.C.: National Black Child Development Institute, 1985).

"Early Childhood Ed Examined," *Education USA*, December 21, 1987.

Kagan, Sharon Lynn, "Four-Year-Olds and the Schools," *Education Week*, December 11, 1985.

Marx, Anne, and Michelle Seligson, *The Public School Early Childhood Study: The State Survey* (New York: Bank Street College of Education, 1988).

Mitchell, Anne, *The Public School Early Childhood Study: The Case Studies* (New York: Bank Street College of Education, 1988).

Mitchell, Anne, *The Public School Early Childhood Study: The District Survey* (New York: Bank Street College of Education, 1988).

Morado, Carolyn, "Prekindergarten Programs for Four-Year-Olds: State

Education Agency Initiatives," policy perspective (Washington, D.C.: National Association for the Education of Young Children, 1986).

Nienhuis, Marleen, "Schools Gaining Ground in Competition to Sponsor Early-Childhood Programs," *Education Week*, November 26, 1986.

Robinson, Sandra L., "Are Public Schools Ready for Four-Year-Olds?" *Principal*, May 1987.

"Safeguards: Guidelines for Establishing Programs for Four-Year-Olds in the Public Schools" (Washington, D.C.: National Black Child Development Institute, 1987).

Schweinhart, Lawrence J., *A School Administrator's Guide to Early Childhood Programs* (Ypsilanti, Mich.: High/Scope Press, 1988).

"Take a Giant Step: An Equal Start in Education for All New York City Four-Year-Olds" (Early Childhood Education Commission, 250 Broadway, Room 1412-14, New York, NY 10007, March 1986).

Zigler, Edward F., "Should Four-Year-Olds Be in School?" *Principal*, May 1986.

CHAPTER 2

Head Start

Koppelman, Jane, and Lori Durso, "Head Start and the Public Schools— The Time to Talk Is Now," *Report on Preschool Programs*, Special Report, April 16, 1986.

Koshel, Jeff, "The Role Played by Head Start in Serving Disadvantaged Children—Implications for States," issue brief (Washington, D.C.: National Governors' Association, February 1986).

Infant and Toddler Care

Belsky, Jay, "Infant Day Care: A Cause for Concern?" **Zero to Three,** September 1986.

"The Crisis in Infant and Toddler Child Care" (Washington, D.C.: Ad Hoc Day Care Coalition, 1985).

Phillips, Deborah, et. al., "Selective Review of Infant Day Care Research: Cause for Concern!" *Zero to Three*, March 1987.

Kindergarten

A Place Called Kindergarten (Urbana, Ill.: Clearinghouse on Elementary and Early Childhood Education, 1988).

Educational Research Service, "A Kindergarten Survey," *Principal*, May 1986.

"Full-Day or Half-Day Kindergarten?"

ERIC/EECE Newsletter (Urbana, Ill.: Educational Resources Information Center/Elementary and Early Childhood Education, Vol. 17, No. 4, 1985).

Moyer, Joan, Harriet Egertson, and Joan Isenberg, "The Child-Centered Kindergarten," Association for Childhood Education International position paper, *Childhood Education*, April 1987.

"Unacceptable Trends in Kindergarten Entry and Placement," National Association of Early Childhood Specialists in State Departments of Education position statement (Lincoln, Neb.: NAECS/SDE, 1988).

Extended Day (Before- and After-School) Care

Baden, Ruth Kramer, et. al., *School-Age Child Care: An Action Manual* (Boston: Auburn House Publishing Company, 1982).

Cohen, Abby J., *School-Age Child Care: A Legal Manual for Public-School Administrators* (Wellesley, Mass.: School-Age Child Care Project, 1984).

Employer-Sponsored Care

Galinsky, Ellen, *Investing in Quality Child Care: A Report for AT&T* (New York: Bank Street College of Education, 1986).

Galinsky, Ellen, D. Hughes, and M. Shinn, *The Corporate Work and Family Life Study* (New York: Bank Street College of Education, 1986).

"Information Kit on Employer-Assisted Child Care" (Washington, D.C.: National Association for the Education of Young Children, 1986).

Other Types of Care

Bridgman, Anne, "Intervention in the Early Years: Initiatives for Handicapped Preschoolers Lift Hopes, Leave Unanswered Questions," *Education Week*, December 18, 1985.

Fraas, Charlotte Jones, "Preschool Programs for the Education of Handicapped Children: Background, Issues, and Federal Policy Options" (Washington, D.C.: Congressional Research Service, Library of Congress, March 17, 1986).

Lindner, Eileen, Mary Mattis, and J. Rogers, "When Churches Mind the Children" (Ypsilanti, Mich.: High/Scope Press, 1983).

Licensing, Regulating, and Insuring Early Childhood Programs

"A Guide to Child Care Regluations in (Your State)," booklet, available by state, developed by Work/Family Directions (Washington, D.C.: National Association for the Education of Young Children, undated).

"Insurance Crunch Easing, But Not Ending," *Child Care Information Exchange*, March 1988, p. 8.

"Licensing and Other Forms of Regulation of Early Childhood Programs in Centers and Family Day Care," National Association for the Education of Young Children position statement (Washington, D.C.: NAEYC, 1987).

A Selection of State Reports

"About the Preschool Years: Educational Opportunities in Virginia," Virginia Secretary of Education and the Virginia Department of Education, 1986.

"The Children's Learning Environment: Facilities for the Children in Early Childhood Family Education," Minnesota Department of Education, 1985.

"Early Childhood Education Handbook 1987," Alaska Department of Education, 1987.

"Florida Prekindergarten Early Intervention Program: A Report on the Availability of Prekindergarten Programs in Each School District and a

Five-Year Plan for Statewide Implementation," State Advisory Council on Early Childhood Education, January 1988.

"Growing: Pre-Kindergarten Through 2nd Grade," 2nd edition, Oklahoma Department of Education, 1985.

"Policy on Early Childhood Education," Massachusetts Board of Education, January 1986.

"Public Schools and School-Age Child Care: Making It Happen!" Missouri Department of Elementary and Secondary Education and the Children's Services Commission, 1987.

CHAPTER 3
Program Format and Components

Berk, Hulda, *Early Childhood Education: An Introduction Bridging the Gap* (Buffalo, N.Y.: Prometheus Books, 1988).

Brady, Elizabeth H., and Shirley Hill, "Young Children and Microcomputers: Research Issues and Directions," Research in Review, *Young Children*, March 1984.

Buckleitner, Warren, *1988 Survey of Early Childhood Software* (Ypsilanti, Mich.: High/Scope Press, 1988).

Chall, Jeanne S., *Stages of Reading Development* (New York: McGraw Hill, 1983).

Chall, Jeanne S., "Reading the Early Childhood Education: The Critical Issues," *Principal*, May 1987.

Early Childhood and Literacy Development Committee, "Literacy Development and Pre-First Grade" (Newark, Del.: International Reading Association, undated).

"Facility Design for Early Childhood Programs," resource guide (Washington, D.C.: National Association for the Education of Young Children, 1987).

Fields, Marjorie V., and Deborah V. Hillstead, "Reading Begins With Scribbling," *Principal*, May 1986.

Frost, Joe L., and Sylvia Sunderlin, eds., *When Children Play: Proceedings of International Conference on Play and Play Environments* (Wheaton, Md.: Association for Childhood Education International, 1985).

Greenman, Jim, *Caring Spaces, Learning Places: Children's Environments That Work* (Redmond, Wash.: Exchange Press Inc., 1988).

Haug, Kathleen, "A Guide for Designing the Children's Learning Environment of an Early Childhood Family Education Program and Additional Resources" (White Bear Lake, Minn.: Minnesota Curriculum Services Center, supported by the State of Minnesota Department of Education and the State Board of Vocational Technical Education, 1985).

"The High/Scope Early Childhood Software Award of Excellence for the design of computer software for young children," *High/Scope ReSource*, Spring/Summer 1988.

Honig, Alice S., "Love and Learn: Discipline for Young Children" (Washington, D.C.: National Association for the Education of Young Children, 1985).

Katz, Lilian, "Curriculum for Preschool and Kindergarten," 16-minute video (Washington, D.C.: National Association for the Education of Young Children, 1985).

"The Learning Environment in Early Childhood Education: Guidelines for Organizing, Observing, and Evaluating Programs" (Jefferson City, Miss.: Missouri Department of Elementary and Secondary Education, 1980).

Moyer, Joan, ed., *Selecting Educational Equipment and Materials for School and Home* (Wheaton, Md.: Association for Childhood Education International, 1986).

O'Brien, Shirely, "Child Sexual Abuse: What Are You Going to Do About It?" videotape and audiotape (Wheaton, Md.: Association for Childhood Education International, 1986).

Wilson, LaVisa Cam, and Neith Headley, "Working with Young Children" (Wheaton, Md.: Association for Childhood Education International, 1983).

CHAPTER 4

Developmental Appropriateness

Bredekamp, Sue, ed., *Developmentally Appropriate Practice in Early Childhood Programs Serving Children from Birth Through Age Eight* (Washington, D.C.: National Association for the Education of Young Children, 1987).

"Child-Initiated Learning Activity Is Crucial," fact sheet (Ypsilanti, Mich.: High/Scope Educational Research Foundation, undated).

Day, Barbara, and Kay N. Drake, "Developmental and Experiential Programs: The Key to Quality Education and Care of Young Children," *Educational Leadership,* November 1986.

Elkind, David, "Formal Education and Early Childhood Education: An Essential Difference," *Phi Delta Kappan*, May 1986.

Elkind, David, *Miseducation: Preschoolers at Risk* (New York: Alfred A. Knopf, Inc., 1987).

Galinsky, Ellen, "Promoting Positive Growth in Children Is No Accident," *Index: Child Care* (Child Development Designs, Inc., 3375 Buckingham Trail, West Bloomfield, MI 48033, June 1987).

Kamii, Constance, "Can There Be Excellence in Education Without Knowledge of Child Development?," paper presented at the annual conference of the Chicago Association for the Education of Young Children, February 8-9, 1985.

Schweinhart, Lawrence J., David P. Weikart, and Mary B. Larner, "Consequences of Three Preschool Curriculum Models Through Age 15," *Early Childhood Research Quarterly* (reprints available from Ypsilanti, Mich.: High/Scope Educational Research Foundation, 1986).

Screening and Readiness Testing

Anderson, Kent C., "Early Prevention of School Failure" (ERIC Document 260 508), 1985.

Hills, Tynette Wilson, "Screening for School Entry," *ERIC Digest* (Urbana, Ill.: ERIC Clearinghouse on Elementary and Early Childhood Education, 1987).

Meisels, Samuel J., *Developmental Screening in Early Childhood: A Guide*, revised edition (Washington, D.C.: National Association for the Education of Young Children, 1985).

CHAPTER 5

Teachers

Futrell, Mary Hatwood, "Public Schools and Four-Year-Olds: A Teacher's View" (Washington, D.C.: National Education Association, undated).

"In Whose Hands: A Demographic Fact Sheet on Child Care Providers" (Washington, D.C.: National Association for the Education of Young Children, 1985).

"Nomenclature, Salaries, Benefits, and the Status of the Early Childhood Profession," National Association for the Education of Young Children position statement (Washington, D.C.: NAEYC, 1984).

Whitebook, Marcy, "The Teacher Shortage: A Professional Precipice," *Young Children*, March 1986.

Training, Certification, and Staff Development

"Early Childhood Teacher Education Guidelines for Four- and Five-Year Programs," National Association for the Education of Young Children position statement (Washington, D.C.: NAEYC, 1982).

"Guidelines for Early Childhood Education Programs in Degree Granting Institutions," National Association for the Education of Young Children position statement (Washington, D.C.: NAEYC, 1985).

Hitz, Randy, "Certification of Teachers of Young Children" (Salem, Or.: Oregon Department of Education, 1986).

"Improving Child Care Through the Child Development Associate (CDA) Program" (Washington, D.C.: CDA National Credentialing Program, undated).

Logue, Mary Ellin, Brenda Krause Eheart, and Robin Lynn Leavitt, "Staff Training: What Difference Does It Make?" *Young Children*, July 1986.

"Preparation of Early Childhood Teachers," Association for Childhood Education International Teacher Education Committee (Wheaton, Md.: ACEI, 1983).

CHAPTER 6

Parental Involvement

Becher, Rhoda, "Parent Involvement: A Review of Research and Principles of Successful Practice" (ERIC Document 247 032), 1984.

White, Burton L., "Education Begins at Birth," *Principal*, May 1987.

CHAPTERS 7 AND 8

Program Start-Up

Collins, Lee, "How to Offer Early Childhood Education on a Baby Budget," *American School Board Journal*, January 1987.

"How to Plan and Start a Good Early Childhood Program," brochure (Washington, D.C.: National Association for the Education of Young Children, undated).

Kristensen, Nancy K., "A Guide for Developing Early Childhood Family Education Programs" (Minnesota Council on Quality Education, 722 Capitol Square Building, St. Paul, Minn. 55101, 1988).

McCormick, Kathleen, "Don't Rush Into the Preschool Business Without Reading This," *American School Board Journal*, June 1986.

Schweinhart, Lawrence J., "When the Buck Stops Here: What It Takes to Run Good Early Childhood Programs," *High/Scope ReSource*, Fall 1987.

Swick, Kevin J., and Kathryn Castle, eds., *Acting on What We Know: Guidelines for Developing Effective Programs for Young Children* (Little Rock, Ark.: Southern Association on Children Under Six, 1985).

Day-to-Day Management of Programs

Brown, J.F., ed., *Administering Programs for Young Children* (Washington, D.C.: National Association for the Education of Young Children, 1984).

Morgan, Gwen, *Managing the Day Care Dollars: A Financial Handbook*, 2nd revised edition (Mt. Rainier, Md.: Gryphon House, 1986).

Schweinhart, Lawrence J., and David P. Weikart, eds., "Quality in Early Childhood Programs: Four Perspectives," Early Childhood Policy Paper No. 3 (Ypsilanti, Mich. High/Scope Educational Research Foundation, 1985).

Evaluation

Bredekamp, Sue, ed., *Accreditation Criteria and Procedures of the National Academy of Early Childhood Programs* (Washington, D.C.: National Association for the Education of Young Children, 1987).

Epstein, Ann S., "A No-Frills Approach to Program Evaluation," *High/Scope ReSource*, Winter 1988.

Selected Periodicals for the Early Childhood/Child Care Field

The ACEI Exchange (newsletter published monthly from September through June by the Association for Childhood Education International, 11141 Georgia Ave., Suite 200, Wheaton, MD 20902)

Child Care Information Exchange (bimonthly magazine on management for program administrators, P.O. Box 2890, Redmond, WA 98073)

Childhood Education (journal published bimonthly from October through June by the Association for Childhood Education International, 11141 Georgia Ave., Suite 200, Wheaton, MD 20902)

Dimensions (journal for teachers published by the Southern Association on Children Under Six, P.O. Box 5403, Brady Station, Little Rock, AR 72215)

Early Childhood Research Quarterly (quarterly publication on research sponsored by the National Association for the Education of Young Children in cooperation with the ERIC Clearinghouse on Elementary and Early Childhood Education, Ablex Publishing Corporation, 355 Chestnut St., Norwood, NJ 07648)

The Head Start Bulletin: National Resource Exchange (published six times yearly to facilitate an exchange of training and technical assistance information and ideas among Head Start programs and agencies, Presidential Building, Suite 863, 6525 Belcrest Road, Prince George Center, Hyattsville, MD 20782)

High/Scope ReSource (newspaper for educators published three times per year by the High/Scope Press, a division of the High/Scope Educational Research Foundation, 600 North River St., Ypsilanti, MI 48197)

Journal of Research in Childhood Education (journal of recent research published biannually, spring and fall, by the Association for Childhood Education International, 11141 Georgia Ave., Suite 200, Wheaton, MD 20902)

Principal (monthly journal of the National Association of Elementary School Principals, 1615 Duke St., Alexandria, VA 22314, selected issues focus on early childhood education)

Report on Preschool Programs (biweekly newsletter on programs for early childhood development, published by Capitol Publications, Inc., 1300 North 17th St., P.O. Box 9673, Arlington, VA 22209).

School Age NOTES (bimonthly newsletter for teachers and directors, P.O. Box 120674, Nashville, TN 37212)

Six Months to Six Years (published five times yearly, for those involved in the preschool field, Crescent Park Press, Box 448, Eureka Springs, Ark. 72632)

Young Children (bimonthly journal published by the National Association for the Education of Young Children, 1834 Connecticut Ave. N.W., Washington, D.C. 20009)

Appendix III

Sample Health Forms

SAMPLE HEALTH RECORD

To be completed by parents and annually updated by teacher.
This form must follow the pupil when transferred.

I. PERSONAL DATA

NAME _____
      (Last)   (First)   (Middle)   (Nickname)

BIRTH DATE VERIFICATION _____
                                    Mo/Day/Year

SEX: ☐ Male   ☐ Female

SOCIAL SECURITY NUMBER _____

RACE: ☐ American Indian ☐ Asian ☐ Black ☐ Hispanic ☐ White
      ☐ Other _____

(Use Pencil Only)

PUPIL ADDRESS _____

P.O. Box or Route _____

Street or Road _____

City _____ State _____ Zip Code _____

PARENT(S) or GUARDIAN: _____

FATHER (STEPFATHER) _____

Address _____

Phone No. _____

MOTHER (STEPMOTHER) _____

Address _____

Phone No. _____

II. HEALTH INFORMATION
(Sample Health record, cont.)

IN CASE OF EMERGENCY:

CALL: _____

Phone No. _____

PHYSICIAN: _____

Phone No. _____

DENTIST: _____

Phone No. _____

Do you have any concerns about your child's:

1. HEALTH ☐ Yes ☐ No

If yes, explain: _____

2. BEHAVIOR ☐ Yes ☐ No

If yes, explain: _____

3. ABILITY TO GET ALONG WITH OTHERS ☐ YES ☐ NO

If, yes, explain: _____

Does your child require health care (i.e. physician, health department, etc.)

On a regular basis? ☐ Yes ☐ No

Only when needed? ☐ Yes ☐ No

Usual health care provider: _____

Name _____

Address _____

Telephone # _____

Has your child received examinations or treatment other that provided by his/her primary health care provider? ☐ Yes ☐ No

If yes, explain: _____

Provider/Agency _____

Address _____

Approximate dates _____

IMMUNIZATIONS

Record of Immunizations (Enter date of EACH dose)

VACCINE_____

DTP _____

OPV _____

MMR _____

MEASLES _____

MUMPS _____

RUBELLA _____

SOURCE: The North Carolina Department of Public Education and the Department of Human Resources.

SAMPLE MEDICAL STATEMENT

(To be completed by doctor)

This is to certify that I have examined

_____ on _____
(child's name)   (date)

and have found that he/she:

1) has had the immunizations required by Section 3313.671 of the Revised Code for admission to school, or has had the immunizations required by the state department of health for infants and toddlers, or is to be exempted from these requirements for medical reasons.

   Immunization Record. Enter month/day/year of each immunization.

   DTP: 1 _____ 2 _____ 3 _____ 4 _____

   Polio: 1 _____ 2 _____ 3 _____ 4 _____

   Measles, mumps, rubella—usually combined as MMR.

   If separate, measles _____, mumps _____,

   rubella _____.

   The 5th DTP and 4th polio are normally administered just prior to kindergarten.

2) based upon his or her medical history and physical condition at the time of this examination, is free from apparent communicable disease and is in suitable condition to receive child day care.

Physician's Signature _____

Street Address _____

Child's Birthdate _____

City, State and Zip Code _____

Telephone Number _____

Date Sent _____

Date Received _____

SOURCE: The Fairview Park Day Care Center, Fairview Park, Ohio

SAMPLE INCIDENT/ACCIDENT/INJURY REPORT

I. Name of Injured Child _____

   Birthdate of Child _____

   Age _____

   Date of Incident _____

   Time of Incident _____

II. Description of Incident

   1. Describe the Incident_____

   _____

   _____

   _____

   _____

   _____

   2. Describe the area of the child's body that was injured. (for example; bruised right knee)

   _____

   3. What was the child doing when the incident happened?

   _____

   4. Where in the facility did it happen?

   _____

5. How did the incident happen?

   _____

6. Give the names of the child care staff member(s) supervising child at the time of the incident.

   _____

7. How did the child respond after the incident?

   _____

8. Was first aid given or some other action taken? ☐ Yes ☐ No

   If yes, by whom? _____

   Describe _____

   _____

   _____

III. Signatures

Signature of Person completing the form _____

Signature of Administrator _____

Date _____

IV. Parent Notification

Parent called ☐ Yes ☐ No

Signature of Staff _____

(sample incident/accident report continued)

Comments _____

_____

_____

Parent notified when picking up child ☐ Yes ☐ No

Signature of Staff _____

Comments _____

_____

_____

V. Parent Signature

This is to confirm that I have received a copy of this report on

_____

Date _____ Parent Signature _____

SOURCE: The Fairview Park Day Care Center, Fairview Park, Ohio

Appendix IV

The AASA Survey on Early Childhood Education

In the spring of 1988, the American Association of School Administrators surveyed a sample of its membership on the issues of early childhood education and child care. The survey, mailed to 1,200 AASA members, drew 264 responses. Their comments throw considerable light on the viewpoints, policies, and practices of America's school administrators.

Are Schools Doing Enough?

Administrators responding to the AASA survey were evenly divided over whether their schools are doing enough to provide early childhood programs. Half said their schools are not doing enough—mostly because of funding constraints. The other half said enough is being done—either in light of funding constraints or because of their belief that preschool and child care programs are not the schools' responsibility.

Respondents who said their schools were *not doing enough* included officials whose districts offer no programs and those whose schools offer programs but, they said, could offer more. "We have barely scratched the surface. The need is profound," noted a superintendent whose district offers some prekindergarten programs. Said another: "There is always more you can do." In addition to financial constraints, they cited inadequate facilities and staff limitations as roadblocks to expansion.

Among those who said their schools were *doing enough*, respondents fell into three categories. Some said existing early childhood programs (ranging from classes for new parents to preschool for 3- to 5-year-olds) met the community's needs. "We serve developmentally delayed 4-year-olds in an exemplary preschool program," said Judy Spiegel, director of special programs for the **Milford, Delaware, School District.** "In addition, we presently have a pilot program for 4-year-olds who are not at risk."

Others noted that although their schools do not have preschool programs or do not have many programs, they are doing enough because early childhood education is not the schools' responsibility. "I think schools are responsible for enough 'extra' or 'outside' school functions without now becoming a day care or babysitting service," noted one Michigan superintendent. Said a South Carolina assistant superintendent: "We are educators, not family or child care agencies."

A considerable number of respondents fell between these two groups, explaining that while their schools do not offer preschool programs, they are doing as much as they can with small budgets. "Given present federal and state funding, we cannot continue to expand special programs at the expense of general education!" said LeRoy Hooks, superintendent of **Prophetstown/Lyndon Community Unit School District 3 in Prophetstown, Illinois.** "The community is entitled only to the programs and levels that they are willing to pay for!" Added an Ohio superintendent: "How can I think about an early childhood education program when proper financial support for the present school program is inadequate?"

Before- and After-School Care

Opinion was considerably less divided over the issue of before- and after-school care. Most respondents registered their firm belief that this type of care is not the schools' responsibility. Instead, they suggested, it belongs with families, churches and synagogues, the community, and private providers. "We're a small district," said Nathan Lee, superintendent of the 1,000-student **Grand Saline, Texas, Independent School District.** "We do not want to get into day care."

Explained Gregory Cox, superintendent of **South Lemhi School District** in **Ladore, Idaho:** "We don't provide it and I firmly believe that parents have to find a way to have their children under their care outside of school hours. I don't believe it is a public responsibility. We need to turn around this Spartan concept of community child care. Schools will *never* be able to replace families in providing those key elements to our continued existence."

Among those administrators who said their schools offer extended-day care, most described after-school programs; some spotlighted early-morning programs as an area in need of development. A few respondents said their schools help parents, religious groups, and others in the community by providing space or transportation. Several others noted the problem of latchkey children, linking difficulties in learning to the time children spend in self-care.

The Need to Recognize Trends, Community Needs

Assessing the survey's results, some experts in the field of early education tried to explain why a number of respondents expressed views that differ from the public at large and others involved in the field. Lawrence Schweinhart, director of the Voices for Children project of the High/Scope Educational Research Foundation, says much of the policy formation and dissemmination in the field has taken place on the state level, leaving district-level administrators out of the process.

In addition, he notes, while many education associations and organizations have begun to address the early childhood/preschool issue, dissemmination to members has been spotty. Schweinhart advises administrators to take into consideration the needs of the community, and to recognize that state legislators are moving ahead in many areas to institute school-based programs.

Others speculate that another reason for the responses may relate to the fact that many superintendents are older males who have not had to deal with child care in their own lives and hence are less likely to advocate for it in their schools.

"The Public School Early Childhood Study," conducted by Bank Street College of Education and Wellesley College's Center for Research on Women, cited superintendents' views and current operational facts as contributors to the unlikelihood that public schools will rapidly expand services to support families to support themselves. And it's important to note that, even when administrators support early childhood programs, they are sometimes unable to get board approval for those programs.

Despite these findings, a significant number of school administrators, especially those who recognize demographic forces and community needs and watch closely the political climate in their states and towns, are well aware of the need for high quality early childhood development programs. For them, funding constraints are what stand in the way of instituting and expanding programs.

Samuel Sava, executive director of the National Association of Elementary School Principals, understands this position. "Superintendents deal daily with using existing resources for the K–12 program," he says. "Now you're asking them to stretch that even further for prekindergarten programs and they're saying, 'We can't do it.'"

There is a growing belief that true advocates for children have no choice but to provide programs—and fight for funding at every level. Administrators must come to terms with the needs of current society and the role educators can play in helping provide positive experiences for young children.

ABOUT THE AUTHOR

Anne Bridgman is an education writer specializing in early childhood education and child care issues. A graduate of the University of Virginia, Anne worked for *Education Week*, the national independent newspaper, for five years as a reporter and editor. It was there that she began writing about the nation's growing interest in early childhood issues. She also has written for *The American School Board Journal, The Boston Globe, Child, Childhood Education, The Christian Science Monitor, The Chronicle of Higher Education, The Executive Educator, Sesame Street Magazine's Parents' Guide,* and *Phi Delta Kappan.*

ACKNOWLEDGMENTS

Early Childhood Education and Child Care was published as a result of the American Association of School Administrators' firm belief in the importance of a good early start for all children. Our research and the advice of experts confirms the fact that the need for developmentally appropriate child care, preschool, and kindergarten programs is great in light of our changing society.

Special thanks go to the 284 school leaders who took the time to respond to AASA's survey and to describe successful early childhood programs in their districts. Their examples and ideas provide excellent models for administrators involved in starting or maintaining programs for young children. AASA also expresses its appreciation to the numerous education organizations and early childhood experts whose research and writings formed the basis for this work.

Also contributing expertise to this publication were Larry Schweinhart, director of the Voices for Children project of the High/Scope Educational Research Foundation; Sam Sava, executive director of the National Association of Elementary School Principals; Lucy Prete Martin, director of publications and editor with the Association for Childhood Education International; Roger Neugebauer, editor of "Child Care Information Exchange"; Barbara Willer, director of policy for the National Association for the Education of Young Children; and Deborah Phillips, assistant professor of psychology at the University of Virginia.

Ann Bridgman, an education writer specializing in early childhood education and child care issues, served as the author of this book. The manuscript was edited by AASA Assistant Communications Director Luann Fulbright and Associate Editor Leslie Payne, who also oversaw its production. AASA Associate Executive Director Gary Marx, who served as project director, perceived the need for a comprehensive, practical book pooling knowledge of early childhood education.